Marie Belloc Lowndes

H. R. H. - The Prince of Wales

An account of his career, including his birth, education, travels, marriage and home

life; and philanthropic, social and political work

Marie Belloc Lowndes

H. R. H. - The Prince of Wales
An account of his career, including his birth, education, travels, marriage and home life; and philanthropic, social and political work

ISBN/EAN: 9783337211851

Printed in Europe, USA, Canada, Australia, Japan

Cover: Foto ©ninafisch / pixelio.de

More available books at **www.hansebooks.com**

H. R. H.

THE PRINCE OF WALES

An Account of his Career, including his Birth,
Education, Travels, Marriage and Home
Life ; and Philanthropic, Social
and Political Work

New York
D. APPLETON AND COMPANY
1898

PREFACE

THE aim of this Book is to give an accurate record of the life of the Prince of Wales. No previous attempt has been made to present even a partially complete biography of His Royal Highness, although isolated portions of the Prince's manifold activities have been treated of by various writers. Thus the author of the present work acknowledges considerable indebtedness to Sir W. H. Russell's fascinating volumes on the Prince and Princess of Wales's tour in the East and the Prince of Wales's tour in India (from which the Illustrations on pp. 99 and 105 are reproduced); to Sir H. C. Burdett's " Prince, Princess, and People," which deals mainly with the philanthropic side of the Prince's life and character; and to Mr. A. H. Beavan's "Marlborough House and its Occupants." A large number of memoirs have also been consulted, including those of the Prince Consort, Baron Stockmar, Mr. Charles Greville, Dr. Norman Macleod, Canon Kingsley, Dean Stanley, and Archbishop Magee.

CONTENTS

CHAPTER I
BIRTH AND EARLY EDUCATION — PAGE 1

CHAPTER II
THE PRINCE'S VISIT TO CANADA AND THE UNITED STATES . 21

CHAPTER III
LIFE AT CAMBRIDGE AND THE CURRAGH—DEATH OF THE PRINCE CONSORT—THE PRINCE OF WALES'S TOUR IN THE EAST 32

CHAPTER IV
THE PRINCE OF WALES'S MARRIAGE 42

CHAPTER V
EARLY MARRIED LIFE . . . 59

CHAPTER VI
ILLNESS OF THE PRINCESS—ROYAL VISIT TO IRELAND—CONTINENTAL AND EASTERN TOUR . 71

CHAPTER VII
THE PRINCE'S ILLNESS 81

CHAPTER VIII

1873-1875 . . . 90

CHAPTER IX

THE PRINCE OF WALES'S TOUR IN INDIA . 95

CHAPTER X

QUIET YEARS OF PUBLIC WORK, 1876-87—VISIT TO IRELAND—THE QUEEN'S JUBILEE . . . 111

CHAPTER XI

SILVER WEDDING OF THE PRINCE AND PRINCESS OF WALES—ENGAGEMENT AND MARRIAGE OF PRINCESS LOUISE OF WALES . . 122

CHAPTER XII

THE BACCARAT CASE—BIRTH OF LADY ALEXANDRA DUFF—THE PRINCE OF WALES'S FIFTIETH BIRTHDAY—ILLNESS OF PRINCE GEORGE OF WALES 130

CHAPTER XIII

THE DUKE OF CLARENCE AND AVONDALE . 134

CHAPTER XIV

1893-1897 142

CHAPTER XV

SANDRINGHAM . 154

CHAPTER XVI

LIFE IN LONDON . 164

CONTENTS xi

CHAPTER XVII

PAGE
PERSONAL CHARACTERISTICS 173

CHAPTER XVIII

PERSONAL CHARACTERISTICS—*continued* 181

CHAPTER XIX

THE PRINCE AS A SPORTSMAN — THE TURF — PERSIMMON'S DERBY — THE DERBY-DAY DINNER — HUNTING — SHOOTING — DEER-STALKING — YACHTING 189

LIST OF ILLUSTRATIONS

	PAGE
H.R.H. The Prince of Wales	*Frontispiece*
The Prince of Wales and the Princess Royal in 1842	xvi
The Queen, the Princess Royal, and the Prince of Wales	3
The Prince of Wales	5
The Prince of Wales at the Age of Three	6
The Christening of the Prince of Wales	7
The Rev. Henry Mildred Birch, the Prince's First Tutor	8
The Queen, the Prince Consort, and their Children	9
The Prince of Wales at the Age of Eight, and the Duke of Saxe-Coburg-Gotha at the Age of Five	10
The Landing of the Queen at Aberdeen in 1849	11
The Prince in 1847	13
Sketching at Loch Laggan—The Queen with the Prince of Wales and the Princess Royal	14
Queen Victoria and the young Prince	15
The Prince in 1859	17
Christ Church, Oxford	19
The Tour in Canada and the United States, 1860	21
The Duke of Newcastle	22
The Prince's Landing at Montreal	24
The Prince of Wales laying the Last Stone of the Victoria Bridge over the St. Lawrence	25
The Grand Ball given at the Academy of Music, New York	29
Trinity College, Cambridge	32
The Prince in 1861	34
Dean Stanley	38

xiv THE PRINCE OF WALES

	PAGE
The Prince of Wales's Reception by Said Pacha, Viceroy of Egypt, at Cairo	39
The Princess Alexandra of Denmark	43
The Prince on Coming of Age	45
The Princess in 1863	47
The Princess	49
The Marriage of the Prince and Princess	51
A Contemporary Design for the Marriage of the Prince and Princess	53
On the Wedding Day	57
The Princess in 1863	61
The Princess in 1864	63
The Princess with the Baby Prince Albert Victor	65
The Prince, the Princess, and Prince Albert Victor	67
The Queen with Prince Albert Victor	69
The Prince at the Age of Twenty-Three	73
The Queen, the Princess of Wales, and Princess Helena	75
Thanksgiving Day, 1872 : The Scene at Temple Bar	86
Thanksgiving Day, 1872 : The Procession up Ludgate Hill	88
The Queen, with the Princes Albert Victor and George, and the Princess Victoria ot Wales	91
The Prince's Indian Tour, 1875	95
Embarkation on Board the *Serapis* at Brindisi	99
The Prince's Visit to the Cawnpore Memorial	105
The Prince in 1876	109
The Prince in 1879	113
The Prince in 1882	117
The Princess of Wales in her Robes as Doctor of Music	119
The Duchess of Fife and the Princesses Victoria and Maud	125
The Duke of Fife	127
The Duke of Clarence	135
The Princess of Wales	139
The Prince and Princess of Wales, with the Duchess of Fife and Lady Alexandra Duff	143
The Queen and the Duke and Duchess of York	145
The Prince in Admiral's Undress Uniform	148
The Prince as Grand Master of the Knights-Hospitallers of Malta, at the Duchess of Devonshire's Ball	150
The Duke of York in his Robes as a Knight of St. Patrick	151
The Duchess of York	152

LIST OF ILLUSTRATIONS

	PAGE
The Norwich Gate at Sandringham	154
The East Front, Sandringham	156
Sandringham from the Grounds	158
The Princess's Dairy at Sandringham	160
The Kennels, Sandringham	161
The Princess with her Favourite Dogs	162
Marlborough House from the South-west	164
Marlborough House : the Drawing-Room	166
Garden Party at Marlborough House, July 1881	169
Marlborough House : the Salon	171
The Prince of Wales as Colonel of the 18th Hussars	175
The Duke of Connaught and the Prince of Wales	179
Sir Francis Knollys	184
The Prince as Admiral	187
Mr. John Porter and Mr. Richard Marsh, the Prince's Past and Present Trainers, and John Watts, his Jockey	189
The Egerton House Training Stables, Newmarket	191
The Prince's Derby, 1896	192
The Prince as a Sportsman in 1876	196
The *Britannia*	198
The Prince in Yachting Costume	199

THE PRINCE OF WALES AND THE PRINCESS ROYAL IN 1842
From the Painting by Sir W. C. Ross, A.R.A.

CHAPTER I

BIRTH AND EARLY EDUCATION

THE PRINCE OF WALES was born on 9th November 1841, at Buckingham Palace. The Duke of Wellington, who was in the Palace at the time, is said to have asked the nurse, Mrs. Lily, "Is it a boy?" "It's a *Prince*, your Grace," answered the justly offended woman.

The news was received with great enthusiasm throughout the country, and the Queen and Prince Albert had thousands of letters and telegrams of congratulation not only through official sources at home and abroad but from many of Her Majesty's humblest subjects all over the world. *Punch* celebrated the event in some verses beginning—

> Huzza! we've a little Prince at last,
>   A roaring Royal boy;
> And all day long the booming bells
>   Have rung their peals of joy.
>
> And the little park guns have blazed away,
>   And made a tremendous noise,
> Whilst the air has been filled since eleven o'clock
>   With the shouts of little boys.

Even at the moment of his birth the eldest son of the Sovereign became *ipso facto* Duke of Cornwall, and before the Prince was four weeks old he was created Prince of Wales and Earl of Chester by Royal Patent, as the former of these titles never passes by merely hereditary right, but is subject to fresh creation for each holder of the title.

As a matter of fact the title of Duke of Cornwall has always been held by the eldest son of the Sovereign for many centuries, and at the moment of his birth the Prince became entitled to the revenues of the Delectable Duchy, of which the rentals and royalties come to over £60,000 a year. His Royal Highness is also Duke of Rothesay and Duke of Saxe-Coburg-Gotha. He is Prince of Saxony, Earl of Chester, Earl of Carrick, Earl of Dublin, and Baron Renfrew, and he also enjoys the picturesque title of Lord of the Isles.

A little less than a month after the birth of her eldest son the Queen wrote to her uncle, Leopold I., King of the Belgians : " I wonder very much who my little boy will be like. You will understand how fervent are my prayers, and I am sure everybody's must be, to see him resemble his father in every respect, both in body and mind."

The christening of the Prince of Wales took place on 25th January 1842, in St. George's Chapel, Windsor, for although Royal baptisms had hitherto been celebrated within the Palace, both the Queen and Prince Albert felt it to be more in harmony with the religious sentiments of the country that the future King should be christened within a consecrated building.

As can be easily understood, the choice of sponsors for the Prince of Wales was a matter of considerable delicacy. Finally the King of Prussia was asked to undertake the office. He accepted the invitation, and arrived in England a few days before the ceremony in which he was to play so important a part. The Prince's other sponsors were his step-grandmother, the Duchess of Saxe-Coburg, represented by the Duchess of Kent; the Duke of Cambridge ; the young Duchess of Saxe-Coburg (Queen Victoria's sister-in-law), represented by the Duchess of Cambridge; Princess Sophia, represented by the Princess Augusta of Cambridge; and Prince Ferdinand of Saxe-Coburg.

Nothing was omitted to make the Prince of Wales's christening a magnificent and impressive ceremony. There was a full choral service, concluding, by the special desire of Prince Albert, with the Hallelujah Chorus. " It is impossible," wrote the Queen in her *Journal*, " to describe how beautiful and imposing the effect of the whole scene was in the fine old chapel, with the banners, the music, and the light shining on the altar." It was significant of the young Queen's native simplicity that the Prince was only christened

BIRTH AND EARLY EDUCATION 3

Albert, after his father, and Edward, after his grandfather, the Duke of Kent.

Both the Queen and Prince Albert soon showed that they were

THE QUEEN, THE PRINCESS ROYAL, AND THE PRINCE OF WALES
From the Painting by S. Cousins, A.R.A.

determined to allow nothing like publicity to come near their nurseries, and the public obtained but few glimpses of the Prince of Wales as a child. Prince Albert's intimate friend and adviser, Baron Stockmar, wrote a year after his birth to one of his friends: "The

Prince, although a little plagued with his teeth, is strong upon his legs, with a calm, clear, bright expression of face." Before he was eighteen months old His Royal Highness had already sat for his portrait several times.

As may be easily imagined, a good deal of interest was taken in the Royal child by those who had an opportunity of seeing him. When the great geologist, Sir Charles Lyell, went to Balmoral, the Queen's eldest son, "a pleasing, lively boy," gave him an account of the conjuring of Anderson, the "Wizard of the North," who had just then shown the Court some marvellous tricks. Said the Prince in an awestruck tone, "He cut to pieces Mamma's pocket-handkerchief, then darned it and ironed it so that it was as entire as ever ; he then fired a pistol, and caused five or six watches to go through Gibbs's head ; but Papa knows how all these things are done, and had the watches really gone through Gibbs's head he could hardly have looked so well, though he was confounded." Gibbs, it should be mentioned, was a footman.

The Prince may be said to have owed his first training to Lady Lyttelton, Mrs. Gladstone's sister, for she filled the post of governess to the Royal children till our future King was six years old.

The Prince of Wales was only seven years old when his parents began anxiously considering what should be the mode of his education, and to whom it should be entrusted. The public showed a great deal of interest in the matter, and a pamphlet was published when the Heir-Apparent was only in his fifth year, entitled *Who should educate the Prince of Wales?* This contribution to the subject was carefully read by both the Queen and Prince Albert, and they applied to a number of their most trusted friends and to the leading statesmen and churchmen of the day for advice on the important question.

Baron Stockmar contributed his views on the education of Princes in a very lengthy memorandum. One thing the shrewd old German physician wrote was well worthy of notice, and that was, that the education of the Royal children ought to be from its very earliest beginning a truly *moral* and a truly *English* one. The Bishop of Oxford, Dr. Wilberforce, and Sir James Clark came to practically the same general conclusions as did Baron Stockmar,

BIRTH AND EARLY EDUCATION 5

namely, that the best way to build up a noble and princely character was to bring it into intelligent sympathy with the best movements of the age.

After some further discussion Prince Albert opened negotiations

THE PRINCE OF WALES
From an old Print published in 1843

with Mr. Henry Birch, the gentleman who was ultimately entrusted with the responsible position of tutor to the future ruler of the British Empire. This young man had been educated at Eton, where he had been captain of the school. He had taken high honours at Cambridge, and had then gone back to Eton as an assistant master.

6   THE PRINCE OF WALES

The Prince Consort had an interview with Mr. Birch in the August of 1848, and was very favourably impressed. Writing to the Duchess of Coburg, he observed : " Bertie will be given over in a few weeks into the hands of a tutor, whom we have found in a Mr. Birch, a young, good-looking, amiable man. . . . It is an important step, and God's blessing be upon it, for upon the good education of

THE PRINCE OF WALES AT THE AGE OF THREE
From the Painting by W. Hensel, in the possession of the German Emperor

Princes, and especially of those who are destined to govern, the welfare of the world in these days greatly depends."

In the same summer the Prince, who, as we have already seen, is Earl of Dublin as well as Earl of Chester, visited Ireland for the first time. He landed with his parents at Queenstown, and received a splendid ovation, which probably laid the foundation of his hearty sympathy with and liking for the Irish character. Curiously enough, the Prince had visited Ireland, Scotland, and Wales, and had made a

very good impression upon the "Celtic fringe" before he was brought before the public notice of his future English subjects.

He made his first official appearance in London on 30th October 1849. It had been arranged that the Queen was to be present at the opening of the Coal Exchange, but she was not able to go as

THE REV. HENRY MILDRED BIRCH, THE PRINCE'S FIRST TUTOR
Photograph by Eastham, Manchester

she was suffering from chicken-pox. Accordingly it was arranged that the Princess Royal and the Prince of Wales should represent their Royal mother.

"Puss and the boy," as the Queen called them, went with their father in State from Westminster to the city in the Royal barge rowed by twenty-six watermen. All London turned out to meet

BIRTH AND EARLY EDUCATION

the gallant little Prince and his pretty sister. Lady Lyttelton, in a letter to Mrs. Gladstone, gives a charming account of the event, and tells how the Prince Consort was careful to put the Prince of Wales forward. Some city dignitary addressed the young Prince as " the pledge and promise of a long race of Kings," and, says Lady Lyttelton, " poor Princey did not seem to guess at all what he meant." In

THE QUEEN, THE PRINCE CONSORT, AND THEIR CHILDREN
From the Painting by Winterhalter

honour of the Royal children a great many quaint old city customs were revived, including a swan barge, and both the Prince of Wales and the Princess Royal seem to have retained a very delightful recollection of their first sight of the City.

It must have been about this time that Miss Alcott, the author of *Little Women*, paid a visit to London, and sent home to her family the following description of the Prince:—" A yellow-haired laddie, very like his mother. Fanny, W., and I nodded and waved as he passed, and he openly winked his boyish eye at us, for Fanny with her yellow curls and wild waving looked rather rowdy, and the poor little Prince wanted some fun."

Two years later the Prince assisted at the opening of the Great Exhibition of 1851 ; and in the same year Mr. Birch retired from

THE PRINCE OF WALES AT THE AGE OF EIGHT, AND THE DUKE OF SAXE-COBURG-GOTHA AT THE AGE OF FIVE
From the Painting by F. Winterhalter

his responsible post, greatly to the sorrow of his young pupil, who was a most affectionate and open-hearted little boy.

In the June of 1852 Viscountess Canning wrote from Windsor Castle : " Mr. Birch left yesterday. It has been a terrible sorrow to the Prince of Wales, who has done no end of touching things since he heard that he was to lose him three weeks ago. He is such an affectionate, dear little boy ; his little notes and presents, which Mr. Birch used to find on his pillow, were really too moving."

THE LANDING OF THE QUEEN AT ABERDEEN IN 1849
From a Painting by Cleland

As was natural, there were many discussions as to who should become the Prince's next tutor. On the recommendation of Sir James Stephen, Mr. Frederick W. Gibbs was appointed. He remained in his responsible position till 1858, and was rarely separated from his Royal pupil during those seven years.

But although so very much attention was devoted to the education and mental training of the Prince, he spent a very happy and unclouded childhood; and, like all the Queen's children, he is very fond of referring to the days spent by him as a boy in his parents' Scotch and English homes, Balmoral, Osborne, and Windsor.

The Baroness Bunsen in her *Memoirs* gives a charming account of a Masque devised by the Royal children in honour of the anniversary of the Queen and the Prince Consort's marriage. The Prince of Wales, then twelve years old, represented Winter. He wore a cloak covered with imitation icicles, and recited some passages from Thomson's *Seasons*. Princess Alice was Spring, scattering flowers; the Princess Royal, Summer; Prince Alfred, Autumn; while Princess Helena, in the *rôle* of St. Helena, the mother of Constantine, who was, according to tradition, a native of Britain, called down Heaven's benedictions on her much-loved parents.

Shortly before this pretty scene took place, the Prince of Wales had made his first appearance in the House of Lords, sitting beside the Queen upon the Throne. It was on this occasion that the addresses of the two Houses in answer to the Queen's Message announcing the beginning of hostilities in the Crimean war were presented, and there is no doubt that the sad and terrible months that followed made a deep and lasting impression on H.R.H. He took the most vivid interest in the fortune of the war, and in March 1855 went with his parents to the Military Hospital at Chatham, where a large number of the wounded had recently arrived from the East.

The popular concern was exhibited in many ingenious and touching ways. An Exhibition was held at Burlington House in aid of the Patriotic Fund, and all the Royal children who were old enough sent drawings and paintings, the Prince's exhibit obtaining the very considerable sum of 55 guineas.

The worst of the terrible struggle was over by the time the Prince of Wales and the Princess Royal accompanied their parents to Paris in the August of the same year. The visit was in many ways historically eventful. Queen Victoria was the first British Sovereign to enter Paris since the days of Henry VI., and the Royal party received a truly splendid reception. The young Prince and his sister, however, were not allowed to be idle, and though they shared

THE PRINCE IN 1847
From the Painting by Winterhalter

to a great extent in the entertainments organised in honour of the Queen and of the Prince Consort, their headquarters remained the whole time in the charming country palace of St. Cloud, and after sight-seeing in Paris all day, they were always driven back there each evening. It is undoubtedly to the impression left by this visit that the Prince of Wales owes his strong affection and liking for France and the French people. When present at a splendid review, held in honour of the Queen, he attracted quite as much attention as any of his elders, for he was dressed in full Highland costume, and remained in the carriage with his mother and the Empress, while the Emperor and the Prince Consort were on horseback.

SKETCHING AT LOCH LAGGAN—THE QUEEN WITH THE PRINCE OF WALES AND THE PRINCESS ROYAL

From the Painting by Landseer, published in 1858

The British Royal party remained in France eight days. The last gala given in their honour was a splendid ball at Versailles, and on this occasion both the Prince of Wales and the Princess Royal were allowed to be present, and sat down to supper with the Emperor and Empress. There had not been a dance given at Versailles since the days of Louis XVI.

One of the most pleasing traits in Napoleon III.'s character

BIRTH AND EARLY EDUCATION 15

was his great liking for children. As was natural, he paid considerable attention to his youthful guests, who both became much attached to him; and later, when he was living at Chislehurst a broken-hearted

QUEEN VICTORIA AND THE YOUNG PRINCE
After the Painting by Thorburn

exile, the Prince of Wales never lost an opportunity of paying him respectful and kindly attentions. Indeed, the Prince of Wales enjoyed his first Continental holiday so heartily, that he begged the Empress to get leave for his sister and himself to stay a little longer after his parents were gone home. When with some embarrassment she replied that the Queen and the Prince Consort would not be able to do without their two children, he exclaimed, "Not do without us! don't fancy that, for there are six more of us at home, and they don't want *us*"; but it need hardly be added that this naïve exclamation did not have the desired effect, and the young people duly returned home with their parents.

A few days later, the Prince Consort, writing to Baron Stockmar, observed: "You will be pleased to hear how well both the children behaved. They have made themselves general favourites, especially the Prince of Wales, *qui est si gentil*." And on the same topic the Prince wrote to the Duchess of Kent: "I am bound to praise the children greatly. They behaved extremely well and pleased everybody. The task was no easy one for them, but they discharged it without embarrassment and with natural simplicity."

When the Prince was fourteen he started on an *incognito* walking tour in the west of England with Mr. Gibbs and Col. Cavendish. His father wrote to Baron Stockmar: "Bertie's tour has hitherto gone off well and seems to interest him greatly." Then followed a short time spent in Germany, the greater portion of which was passed at Königswinter, on the Rhine.

The Prince of Wales was confirmed in April 1858; the Prince Consort gives an interesting account of the ceremony. "They were all three (Lords Palmerston, Russell, and Derby) at the confirmation of the Prince of Wales, which went off with great solemnity, and, I hope, with an abiding impression on his mind. The previous day, his examination took place before the Archbishop and ourselves. Wellesley prolonged it to a full hour, and Bertie acquitted himself extremely well." The day following his confirmation the Prince received the sacrament with his father and mother.

Shortly after a fourteen days' tour in the south of Ireland undertaken by way of recreation, it was arranged that His Royal Highness should take up his residence at White Lodge, Richmond. He accordingly did so, and the suite of rooms that he occupied while there still bears his name. The Queen and the Prince Consort, anxious that he should not be lonely, appointed as his companions three young

BIRTH AND EARLY EDUCATION 17

men slightly older than himself. One was Lord Valletort, the eldest son of the Earl of Mount Edgcumbe; the second, Major Teesdale, who had greatly distinguished himself at Kars, and who remained one of the Prince's most intimate friends till his death; and the third,

THE PRINCE IN 1859
From a Painting by G. Richmond

Major Lindsay of the Scots Fusiliers, who had received the Victoria Cross for his gallantry at Alma and Inkerman.

By Her Majesty's special desire, Charles Kingsley about this time delivered a series of lectures on history to her eldest son, and the Prince remained fondly attached to the famous author of *Westward Ho*, who, till his death, was an honoured guest at Sandringham and at Marlborough House.

c

On 9th November of the same year the Prince of Wales attained his eighteenth year, and became legally heir to the Crown. The Queen wrote him a letter announcing his emancipation from parental control, and he was so touched by its perusal that he brought it to General Wellesley with tears in his eyes, and we have the impartial testimony of Charles Greville as to the character of the epistle, which was, says the famous diarist, "one of the most admirable letters that ever was penned." On the same day he became a Colonel in the Army, and received the Garter, while Colonel Bruce became his governor.

Exactly a month after his birthday, the Prince started on a Continental tour, travelling more or less *incognito* as Baron Renfrew. He was accompanied by Mr. Tarver, who had just been appointed his chaplain and director of studies. The Prince stayed some time in Rome and visited the Pope, but on 29th April 1859 the Prince Consort wrote to Baron Stockmar : "We have sent orders to the Prince of Wales to leave Rome and to repair to Gibraltar." For it was very properly considered, that owing to the Franco-Italian and Austrian imbroglio, it was far better that the heir to the British throne should be well out of the way of international dissensions.

The Prince reached Gibraltar on 7th May, and visited the south of Spain and Lisbon, returning home in the middle of the next month ; and then, after having seen something of the world, he again took up a very serious course of study, this time at Edinburgh. Meanwhile the education and training of the Heir-Apparent was being watched very carefully by the British public, and a good many people began to consider that their future King was being over-educated ; indeed *Punch*, in some lines entitled "A Prince at High Pressure," undoubtedly summed up the popular feeling, not only describing the past, but prophesying, with a great deal of shrewd insight, the future course of the Prince of Wales's studies :

> To the south from the north, from the shores of the Forth,
> Where at hands Presbyterian pure science is quaffed,
> The Prince, in a trice, is whipped to the Isis,
> Where Oxford keeps springs mediæval on draught.

BIRTH AND EARLY EDUCATION

Dipped in grey Oxford mixture (lest *that* prove a fixture),
The poor lad's to be plunged in less orthodox Cam.,
Where dynamics and statics, and pure mathematics,
Will be piled on his brain's awful cargo of cram.

But the Prince seems to have borne his course of study very well, and after his son had been in Edinburgh some three months the Prince Consort wrote to Baron Stockmar: "In Edinburgh I had an Educational Conference with all the persons who were taking

CHRIST CHURCH, OXFORD

part in the education of the Prince of Wales. They all speak highly of him, and he seems to have shown zeal and goodwill. Dr. Lyon Playfair is giving him lectures on chemistry in relation to manufactures, and at the close of each special course he visits the appropriate manufactory with him, so as to explain its practical application. Dr. Schmitz (the Director of the High School of Edinburgh, a German) gives him lectures on Roman history. Italian, German, and French are advanced at the same time; and three times a week the Prince exercises with the 16th Hussars, who are stationed in the city. Mr. Fisher, who is to be the tutor for

Oxford, was also in Holyrood. Law and history are to be the subjects on which he is to prepare the Prince."

The young Prince spent a delightful holiday in the Highlands, and made an expedition up Ben Muichdhui, one of the highest mountains in Scotland. Then, on 9th November, His Royal Highness's nineteenth birthday was celebrated with the whole of his family, for the Princess Royal had arrived from Berlin in order to spend the day with her brother.

The Prince of Wales was at that time very fond of the writings of Sir Walter Scott. He has always been a reader of fiction, French, English, and German, and as a youth he was studious and eager to learn.

On leaving Scotland he went to Oxford, being admitted a member of Christ Church. The Prince seems to have thoroughly enjoyed his life as an undergraduate. He joined freely in the social life of the University, and took part in all the sports, frequently hunting with the South Oxfordshire Hounds.

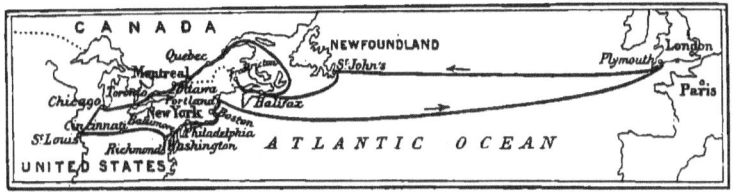

THE TOUR IN CANADA AND THE UNITED STATES, 1860

CHAPTER II

THE PRINCE'S VISIT TO CANADA AND THE UNITED STATES

DURING the Crimean war, Canada, stirred, as seem to have been all the British colonies, by the direful stress of the mother country, levied and equipped a regiment of infantry. In return, the Canadians had asked Her Majesty to visit her American possessions; but it was considered undesirable that the Queen should be exposed to the fatigue and the risks of so long a journey.

Her Majesty was then asked to appoint one of her sons Governor-General of the Dominion, but the extreme youth of all the Princes made that quite out of the question. The Queen, nevertheless, formally promised that when the Prince of Wales was old enough he should visit Canada in her stead. When the Prince was well on in his eighteenth year his parents decided that it was time for this promise to be fulfilled, the more so that it would enable the great railway bridge across the St. Lawrence at Montreal to be opened, and the foundation-stone of the Parliament buildings at Ottawa to be laid, by a Prince of the blood.

The Prince Consort, with the care and forethought which always distinguished him in such matters, made a most careful choice of those who were to accompany his young son. Both the Queen and he felt the greatest confidence in the Duke of Newcastle, and with him Prince Albert arranged all the details of the Prince's Canadian visit. The careful and kindly father forgot nothing that might be needed. Not only did he take special pains to secure that the young Prince should learn something of the history, customs, and prejudices of the Canadian people, but he supplied the Duke with memoranda which might be found useful in drawing up the answers to be made to the addresses which were certain to be presented to the Prince of Wales during his progress through the Dominion. The best proof of the Prince Consort's wisdom is to be found in the fact that every one of these notes afterwards turned out to be simply invaluable, owing

THE DUKE OF NEWCASTLE

to the peculiar aptness with which they had been framed to suit the circumstances of each locality where an address was likely to be received.

When it became known on the American Continent that the Prince of Wales was really coming to Canada, the President of the United States, Mr. Buchanan, wrote to the Queen explaining how cordial a welcome the Prince of Wales would receive at Washington should he extend his visit to the United States.

Her Majesty returned a cordial answer, informing Mr. Buchanan, and through him the American people, that the Prince would return home through America, and that it would give him great pleasure to have an opportunity of testifying to the President in person the kindly feelings which animate the British nation to America. At the same time the American people were told that the future British Sovereign would, from the moment of his leaving British soil, drop all Royal state, and that he would simply travel as " Lord Renfrew." In this again Her Majesty showed her great wisdom, for it would have been extremely awkward for the Prince of Wales, the descendant of George III., to have visited the American Republic in his quality as Heir-Apparent to the British Throne.

After a pleasant but uneventful voyage on board the frigate *Hero*, escorted by H.M.S. *Ariadne*, the Prince of Wales first stepped on Transatlantic soil at St. John's, Newfoundland, on 24th July 1860. The morning was rainy, but the moment His Royal Highness landed the sun shone out, bursting through the clouds, and this was considered by those present to be a very happy omen.

On that day the Prince may be said to have really had his first glimpse of the round of official duties to which he seemed to take naturally and in which he was destined to become so expert.

After the Governor of Newfoundland had been formally presented to the Prince, the Royal party, which comprised, in addition to His Royal Highness, the Duke of Newcastle, General Bruce, and Major Teesdale, went straight to Government House, where the Prince held a reception, and listened to a considerable number of addresses. The day did not end till the next morning, for in the evening a grand ball was given by Sir Alexander Bannerman, and our future King won all hearts by mixing freely with the company, and dancing, not only with the ladies belonging to the Government and official circles, but with the wives and daughters of the fishermen. It was noticed that the Prince was quite remarkably like the portraits of his Royal mother on the British coins, and he displayed not only in Newfoundland, but during the many fatiguing days that followed, the extraordinary tact and admirable breeding which have continually year after year increased the affection with which he is regarded by the British people.

The wife of the then Archdeacon of St. John's, in an interesting letter home, puts on record the impression produced by His Royal Highness in Newfoundland :—

"His appearance is very much in his favour, and his youth and royal dignified manners and bearing seem to have touched all hearts, for there is scarcely a man or woman who can speak of him without tears. The rough fishermen and their wives are quite wild about

THE PRINCE'S LANDING AT MONTREAL
From a contemporary picture in the "Illustrated London News"

him, and we hear of nothing but their admiration. Their most frequent exclamation is, 'God bless his pretty face and send him a good wife.'"

At Halifax the news that his sister, the Princess Royal of Prussia, had given birth to a little daughter met him, and he hastened to write home his affectionate congratulations on the event.

The Prince's tour through Canada may be said to have been one long triumphal procession. It was marred by no unpleasant incident,

VISIT TO CANADA AND THE UNITED STATES 25

in spite of the fact that at Kingston and Toronto the Orangemen tried to induce the Prince to pass under arches decorated with their party symbols and mottoes. Thanks, however, to the Duke ot Newcastle's tact and firmness, the attempt failed, and the incident merely served to illustrate the young Prince's freedom from party bias. Everywhere the Royal visitor produced the happiest impressions, and, thanks to his youth, he was able to endure considerable fatigue without apparently being any the worse for it.

THE PRINCE OF WALES LAYING THE LAST STONE OF THE VICTORIA BRIDGE OVER
THE ST. LAWRENCE
From the "Illustrated London News"

In America "Baron Renfrew's" arrival was awaited with the utmost impatience, and while travelling over the Dominion His Royal Highness was surrounded by American reporters. Indeed, it is said that the Prince of Wales's visit to Canada formed the first occasion on which press telegrams were used to any lavish extent. One enterprising journalist used to transmit to his paper long chapters from the Gospel according to St. Matthew and from the Book of Revelation in order to monopolise the wires while he was gathering material for his daily report of the Royal journey. At a great ball given in Quebec, the Prince tripped and fell with his partner—the article recording this event was headed, *Honi soit qui mal y pense.*

The Royal visit to Montreal is still remembered in Canada. The Prince and his suite arrived there on 25th August, and the Prince, after opening a local exhibition, inaugurating a bridge, holding a review, and attending some native games, danced all night with the greatest spirit, even singing with the band when it struck up his favourite air.

Many little stories were told of His Royal Highness's good-nature and affability. Hearing by accident that an old sailor who had served with Nelson on board the *Trafalgar* had been court-martialled, the Prince begged him off, and asked that he might be restored to his rank in the service.

The Canadian Government provided a number of riding-horses in order that the Prince might see Niagara Falls from several points of view, and he has since often declared that this was one of the finest sights he ever saw in his life. Next day, in the presence of the Royal party and of thousands of spectators, Canadian and American, the famous rope-walker, Blondin, crossed Niagara river upon a rope, walking upon stilts, and carrying a man on his back. After the ordeal was over, Blondin had the honour of being presented to the Prince. The latter, with much emotion, exclaimed, "Thank God, it is all over!" and begged him earnestly not to attempt the feat again, but the famous rope-walker assured His Royal Highness that there was no danger whatever, and offered to carry him across on his back if he would go, but the Prince briefly declined! The Prince seems to have been quite fascinated by the marvellous Falls. On 17th September he insisted on riding over on American ground for a farewell view of Niagara.

The Prince of Wales formally crossed from Canadian territory to the States on the night of 20th September, making his appearance on Republican soil, as had been arranged, as Baron Renfrew. At Hamilton, the last place in Canada where he halted, the Prince made a speech, in the course of which he observed :

" My duties as Representative of the Queen cease this day, but in a private capacity I am about to visit before I return home that remarkable land which claims with us a common ancestry, and in whose extraordinary progress every Englishman feels a common interest."

Great as had been the enthusiasm in Canada, it may be said to have been nothing to the *furore* of excitement produced in America by the Prince of Wales's visit. At Detroit the crowds were so dense that the Royal party could not get to their hotel through the main streets, and had to be smuggled in at a side entrance. The whole city was illuminated; every craft on the river had hung out lamps; and, as one individual aptly put it, "there could not have been greater curiosity to see him if the distinguished visitor had been George Washington come to life again."

Over 50,000 people came out to meet His Royal Highness at Chicago, then a village of unfinished streets, but there, for the first time, the Prince broke down from sheer fatigue, and the Duke of Newcastle decided that it would be better to break the trip from Chicago to St. Louis by stopping at a quiet village, famed even then for the good sport to be obtained in its neighbourhood. Accordingly His Royal Highness had a day's shooting at Dwight's Station. Fourteen brace of quails and four rabbits fell to the Prince's gun. A rather absurd incident marred the complete pleasure of the day. As the Royal party approached a farmhouse an unmistakably British settler appeared at the door and invited every one *excepting the Duke of Newcastle* to enter. "Not you, Newcastle," he shouted; "I have been a tenant of yours, and have sworn that you shall never set a foot on my land." Accordingly the party passed on, and the farmer, though revenged on his old landlord, had to forgo the honour of entertaining Royalty under his roof.

But notwithstanding this *contretemps* the Prince seems to have thoroughly enjoyed his little outing. At one moment, when he was out on the prairie, he and his companions desired to smoke, but nobody had a light. At last a single match was found, but no one volunteered to strike it. Lots were drawn with blades of the prairie grass, and the Prince drew the shortest blade. The others held their coats and hats round him whilst he lighted the match, and he once said that he has never felt so nervous before or since.

On 30th October "Lord Renfrew" reached Washington, and Lord Lyons, the British Minister, introduced him to President Buchanan, and Miss Harriet Lane, the latter's niece and housekeeper. The Prince stayed at the White House, and President James Buchanan, though he could not spare his Royal guest a certain number of *levées* and receptions, did his best to make his visit to the official centre of the American Republic pleasant. During these five days there occurred a most interesting event—the visit of His Royal Highness to Mount Vernon, and the tomb of Washington. A representative of the *Times* gave the following eloquent account of the scene:—

"Before this humble tomb the Prince, the President, and all the party stood uncovered. It is easy moralising on this visit, for there is something grandly suggestive of historical retribution in the reverential awe of the Prince of Wales, the great-grandson of George III., standing bareheaded at the foot of the coffin of Washington. For a few moments the party stood mute and motionless, and the Prince then proceeded to plant a chestnut by the side of the tomb. It seemed, when the Royal youth closed in the earth around the little germ, that he was burying the last faint trace of discord between us and our great brethren in the West."

Doubtless the Prince enjoyed these new experiences a good deal more than did his guides, philosophers, and friends. Political feeling ran high, and the pro-slavery leaders were very anxious to influence public sentiment in Great Britain. They formed the project of taking the Prince of Wales through the South to see slavery under its pleasantest aspect as a paternal institution. After a good deal of discussion between the Duke of Newcastle and Lord Lyons, it was felt better to accept the invitation of some representative Southerners, and accordingly the Prince went a short tour to Richmond; but it may be added that a great slave sale which had been widely advertised was postponed so as not to offend British susceptibilities. The Prince does not seem to have been at all impressed by the slave cities, and he flatly refused to leave his carriage to visit the negro quarters at Haxhall's plantation, and so he returned to Washington, having shown a good deal more common sense than had those about him.

The day that the Prince left Washington for Richmond, President Buchanan wrote a charming letter to the Queen, in which he said,

VISIT TO CANADA AND THE UNITED STATES

speaking of his guest : " In our domestic circle he has won all hearts. His free and ingenuous intercourse with myself evinced both a kind heart and a good understanding."

From Washington the Prince proceeded to Philadelphia, and there, for the first time, His Royal Highness heard Adelina Patti. He was so greatly charmed with her marvellous voice and winning personality, that he begged that she might be presented to him.

THE GRAND BALL GIVEN AT THE ACADEMY OF MUSIC, NEW YORK
From the " Illustrated London News "

The Prince's feelings must have been strangely mixed when he stood in Independence Hall, but he does not appear to have revealed them by making any remark, and after staying a few days in Philadelphia he started for New York, where he received a splendid welcome from Father Knickerbocker, being met at the station by the Mayor, and driven through Broadway to the Fifth Avenue Hotel. Half a million spectators saw him arrive, and so great was the anxiety to see Queen Victoria's eldest son at close quarters, that there was no structure in New York large enough to contain those who thought that they had—and who no doubt had—a right to meet the Prince of Wales at a social function.

At last a building was found capable of containing 6000 people; but, looking to the question of "crinolines and comfort," it was reluctantly decided that not more than 3000 cards of invitation, admitting to the ball and to the supper to follow, should be sent out. Fortunately most of the 3000 guests were important people, and therefore too old to dance. They represented, in both senses of the word, the solid element in New York society, for, as they crowded round the Prince, the floor gave way, and it is a wonder that no serious accident took place. This splendid entertainment, which took place in the old Academy of Music, is still remembered by many elderly Americans. The Prince showed his tact and good taste by frequently changing his partner. For the supper, a special service of china and glass had been manufactured, the Prince's motto, *Ich Dien*, being emblazoned on every piece.

During the five days that the Prince remained in New York, he was the guest of the Mayor and of the Corporation. He seems to have most enjoyed a parade of the Volunteer Fire Department in his honour. There were 6000 firemen in uniform, and all, save those in charge of the ropes and tillers, bore torches. The scene was quite unique, and the Prince, as he looked at the brilliant display in Madison Square, cried repeatedly, "This is for me, this is all for me!" with unaffected glee.

From New York the Prince went on to Albany and Boston, and at the latter place Longfellow, Oliver Wendell Holmes, Emerson, and a number of other notable Americans were presented to him. He visited Harvard College, spent an hour at Mount Auburn, where he planted two trees, and drove out to Bunker's Hill.

Portland was the last place visited by the Prince in the United States, and on 20th October the Royal party set sail for home on board the *Hero*, which was escorted by the *Ariadne*, the *Nile*, and the *Styx*. The voyage home was not as uneventful as had been the voyage out. So anxious were they at Court about the fate of the *Hero*, that two ships of war were sent in search of the frigate and her escort. At last, to every one's great relief, the *Hero* was sighted, and it was ascertained that a sudden storm had driven the boat back from the

VISIT TO CANADA AND THE UNITED STATES

British coast, and the Royal party had been reduced to salt fare, with only a week's provisions in store.

On 9th November the Prince Consort put in his diary : "Bertie's birthday. Unfortunately he is still absent, neither do we hear anything from him." Great, therefore, was the joy of the Queen and Prince Albert when, on 15th November, they received a telegram from Plymouth announcing the safe arrival of their son. That same evening the Prince of Wales arrived at Windsor Castle, being greeted with the warmest affection by his family and friends.

The Queen showed the most vivid interest in all her eldest son's many and varied adventures. Both Her Majesty and the Prince Consort were very much gratified by the way in which the Duke of Newcastle had performed his arduous and delicate task, and, after some consultation, it was decided that the Queen should publicly mark her satisfaction by conferring upon the Duke the Order of the Garter.

TRINITY COLLEGE, CAMBRIDGE

CHAPTER III

LIFE AT CAMBRIDGE AND THE CURRAGH—DEATH OF THE PRINCE CONSORT—THE PRINCE OF WALES'S TOUR IN THE EAST

EARLY in 1861 the Prince of Wales became an undergraduate member of Trinity College, Cambridge. Curiously enough, Dr. Whewell, at that time Master of Trinity, did not think it necessary to make a formal entry of the Royal undergraduate, but in 1883, when His Royal Highness was visiting Cambridge in order to enter his son, the late Duke of Clarence, as a student of Trinity, the Prince expressed the opinion that it was a pity that his own entry had not been properly filled up, and he offered to fill in the blank spaces if the book was brought to him. Accordingly the record may now be found at its proper place in His Royal Highness's own handwriting. His entry is as follows :—

LIFE AT CAMBRIDGE AND THE CURRAGH

Date of entry.	Rank.	Name.
January 18th, 1861.	Nobleman.	Albert Edward Prince of Wales.
Father's Christian Name.	Native Place.	County.
Albert.	London.	Middlesex.
School.	Age.	Tutor.
Private Tutor.	November 9th, 1841.	Admitted by order of the Seniority, Mr. Mathison being his tutor.

The entry immediately preceding the Prince's name is that of the Hon. J. W. Strutt (now Lord Rayleigh), in connection with which the following amusing story is told. A visitor to the library (where the book is kept) having expressed her doubts as to the Prince's intellectual abilities, the librarian showed her the entry, and said: "You may be right in what you say, madam, but allow me to inform you that the Prince comes next to a former Senior Wrangler." The lady's astonishment may be imagined, she being of course ignorant that mere coincidence was the cause of the juxtaposition of the two names.

The position of the Prince in the University was very much that of an ordinary undergraduate, except in one point—that he was, by special favour, allowed to live with his governor, Colonel the Hon. Robert Bruce, about three miles away from Cambridge, in a little village called Madingley.

Charles Kingsley at the Prince Consort's request gave some private lectures to the Prince of Wales. The class was formed of eleven undergraduates, and after the Prince of Wales settled at Madingley, he rode three times a week to Mr. Kingsley's house, twice attending with the class, and once to go through a *résumé* of the week's work alone; and, according to the great writer's biographer, the tutor much appreciated the attention, courtesy, and intelligence of his Royal pupil, whose kindness to him then and in after-life made him not only the Prince's loyal but his most attached servant.

The Prince certainly enjoyed his life at Cambridge. All sorts of stories, perhaps more or less apocryphal, used to be told as to His Royal Highness's University career. He was not allowed quite as much freedom as the ordinary undergraduate, and Colonel Bruce had strict orders never to allow him to make any long journeys unaccompanied. On one occasion the Prince made up his mind that he would like to pay an *incognito* visit to London, and he succeeded in evading the vigilance of those whose duty it was to attend him. His absence, however, was discovered before he could reach town, and to his surprise and mortification he was met at Paddington by the station-master and by two of the Royal servants who had been sent from Buckingham Palace for that purpose.

THE PRINCE IN 1861
Photograph by Silvy

Shortly after his marriage the Prince took his bride to visit Cambridge, and after the usual reception, the Royal pair drove to Madingley, to view His Royal Highness's former residence. On reaching one of the streets on the borders of the town it was found to be barricaded, it being thought that the carriage would proceed by another route. "This is the way I always came," said the Prince, "and this is the way I wish to go now." Forthwith the sightseers were removed and the barricade broken down, but the Prince signified his intention of returning by the other road so that the spectators might not be disappointed.

The Prince remained more or less constantly at Cambridge all the winter of 1861, and it was arranged that during the long vacation he was to go on military duty at the Curragh.

While the Prince was quartered there, the Queen, the Prince Consort, and the young Princesses paid a short visit to Ireland in order to see His Royal Highness in his new character of soldier. On 26th August Her Majesty wrote in her diary:

LIFE AT CAMBRIDGE AND THE CURRAGH 35

"At a little before 3 we went to Bertie's hut, which is in fact Sir George Brown's. It is very comfortable—a nice little bedroom, sitting-room, drawing-room, and good-sized dining-room, where we lunched with our whole party. Colonel Percy commands the Guards, and Bertie is placed specially under him. I spoke to him, and thanked him for treating Bertie as he did, just like any other officer, for I know that he keeps him up to his work in a way, as General Bruce told me, that no one else has done; and yet Bertie likes him very much."

On the following day, which was a Sunday, the Prince Consort, accompanied by the Prince of Wales and Prince Alfred, went with Lord Carlisle to inspect the Dublin prisons.

Prince Albert spent his last birthday, 26th August 1861, with his son in Ireland, and the Prince of Wales accompanied his parents and sisters to Killarney, where they had a very enthusiastic welcome. They travelled on the Prince Consort's birthday. On the 29th the Queen and the Prince, with their younger children, left Ireland, and writing to Baron Stockmar on 6th September the Prince Consort said: "The Prince of Wales has acquitted himself extremely well in the Camp, and looks forward with pleasure to his visit to the manœuvres on the Rhine."

It was during the autumn of this year that the Prince of Wales, during a short visit to Germany, met Princess Alexandra of Denmark for the first time. To the Prince Consort's great annoyance, a whisper of a projected royal alliance between Great Britain and Denmark had got abroad, and with the delicacy and good feeling which always distinguished him, Prince Albert greatly deplored that this should have been so, for had the young Prince and Princess not taken an instant liking to one another, these rumours would have been greatly to be regretted. As it was, the Prince Consort was able to write on 14th October to Baron Stockmar: "The Prince of Wales leaves to-morrow for Cambridge. He came back greatly pleased with his interview with the Princess of Holstein at Speier. . . . His present wish, after his time at the University is up, which it will be at Christmas, is to travel; and we have gladly assented to his proposal to visit the Holy Land. This, under existing circumstances, is the most useful tour he can make, and will occupy him till early in June."

The Prince Consort that same autumn went specially to London in order to inspect the alterations that were being made at Marlborough House, which was then being actively prepared as a residence ; and on the 9th the Queen wrote in her diary : " This is our dear Bertie's twentieth birthday. I pray God to assist our efforts to make him turn out well. . . . All our people in and out of the house came in to dinner. Bertie led me in by Albert's wish, and I sat between him and Albert."

Prince Albert, on 28th November, paid a hurried visit to Cambridge in order to visit the Prince of Wales. The weather was cold and stormy, and he returned to Windsor with a heavy cold.

The next few days were spent by both the Prince Consort and the Queen in considerable anxiety. The seizure of the *Trent* aroused a great deal of bitter public feeling, and the fact that America was convulsed by civil war did not make the position of Great Britain more easy. The Government took a very determined tone, and the Prince Consort, instead of allowing himself to be nursed through his feverish attack, spent some hours in composing and writing a draft, on the burning question of the day, to Lord Russell.

The story of those sad days is well known. As time went on, the Prince grew slightly worse rather than better, but no real danger was apprehended by those nearest and dearest to him, and the Queen would not hear of having the Prince of Wales summoned, until at last Princess Alice, who behaved with extraordinary fortitude and marvellous self-possession, felt that she must send for her eldest brother on her own responsibility. She accordingly did so, and the Prince arrived in time to be present at his much-loved father's death-bed. Although she was herself overwhelmed with bitter grief, it was to the Princess Alice that all turned, for the Queen was so completely overcome that nothing could be referred to her, and it was finally arranged that the Prince of Wales and the Princesses Alice and Helena should accompany their mother to Osborne, where she had consented very reluctantly to go.

The Prince of Wales returned immediately, in order to complete the arrangements for the funeral, and to receive his uncle the Duke of Saxe-Coburg, his brother-in-law the Crown Prince of Prussia, and the other foreign mourners who were to take part in the last sad ceremony.

The funeral took place on 23rd December, the service being held in St. George's Chapel, Windsor. The chief mourner was, of course, the Prince of Wales, who was supported, in the absence of Prince Alfred (Duke of Edinburgh), by Prince Arthur. All those present were deeply moved by the grief of the two young princes. They both hid their faces, and after the coffin had been lowered into the vault the Prince of Wales advanced to take a last look and stood for one moment looking down; then, his fortitude deserting him, he burst into a flood of tears, and was led away by the Lord Chamberlain.

Sad indeed were the days that followed. The effect of the Prince Consort's death on the Prince of Wales's affectionate and sensitive nature was terrible, and those about the Court felt that something must be done to rouse him from his grief.

The Prince Consort had long before decided that his eldest son should begin his life as a grown-up man by making a tour in the Holy Land, and it had also been his earnest wish that His Royal Highness should on that occasion be accompanied by the Rev. Arthur Penrhyn Stanley, who had himself already taken a journey to Jerusalem. Accordingly, when after the Prince Consort's death it was decided to carry out his long-cherished scheme with regard to the Prince of Wales, the Queen made up her mind that she would be guided by his wishes, and General Bruce was commanded to write to Dr. Stanley, but not till he reached Osborne was he actually asked whether he would consent to undertake the responsibility.

Dr. Stanley, though he regarded the proposal with reluctance and misgiving, for he could not bear to leave his aged mother, to whom he was most tenderly devoted, consented to do as the Queen wished. It was ultimately arranged that he should meet the Prince at Alexandria, ascend the Nile with him, and accompany him, not only through the Holy Land, but on the Egyptian portion of the expedition.

On 28th February the Prince, accompanied by General Bruce, Major Teesdale, Captain Keppel, and a small suite, was joined by Dr. Stanley, the party at once proceeding to Cairo. "The

Prince," wrote General Bruce to his sister, "takes great delight in the new world on which he has entered, and Dr. Stanley is a great

DEAN STANLEY
From a Photograph by the Stereoscopic Co.

acquisition." They visited the Pyramids together, and then resumed their voyage, the Prince characteristically persuading Dr. Stanley to read *East Lynne*, a book which had greatly struck his imagination. When recording the circumstance, Dr. Stanley adds :

"It is impossible not to like him, and to be constantly with him brings out his astonishing memory of names and persons. . . . I am more and more struck by the amiable and endearing qualities of the Prince. . . . His Royal Highness had himself laid down a rule that there was to be no shooting to-day (Sunday), and though he

The Prince of Wales's Reception by Said Pacha, Viceroy of Egypt, at Cairo

From the " Illustrated London News"

was sorely tempted, as we passed flocks of cranes and geese seated on the bank in the most inviting crowds, he rigidly conformed to it ; a crocodile was allowed to be a legitimate exception, but none appeared. He sat alone on the deck with me, talking in the frankest manner, for an hour in the afternoon, and made the most reasonable and proper remarks on the due observance of Sunday in England."

A sad event which occurred in March was destined to draw

closer together the ties which were now binding His Royal Highness and his chaplain, for on 23rd March the news was broken to Dr. Stanley that his mother was dead. The Prince of Wales showed the kindest and most tender consideration for his bereaved travelling companion, and was much gratified that Dr. Stanley very wisely made up his mind to continue the journey instead of hurrying home at once.

A few days later the Royal party reached Palestine, and it is interesting to note that this was the first time that the heir to the English throne, since the days of Edward I. and Eleanor, had visited the Holy City. The Prince of Wales landed at Jaffa on 31st March, and both on his entrance into the Holy Land and during his approach to Jerusalem he followed in the footsteps of Richard Cœur de Lion and Edward I. The cavalcade, escorted by a troop of Turkish cavalry, climbed the Pass of Bethhoron, catching their first glimpse of Jerusalem from the spot where Richard is recorded to have hidden his face in his shield, with the words, "Ah, Lord God, if I am not thought worthy to win back the Holy Sepulchre, I am not worthy to see it!"

The Prince, accompanied by Dr. Stanley, carefully explored Jerusalem and its neighbourhood, riding over the hills of Judæa to Bethlehem, walking through the famous groves of Jericho, and staying some time at Bethany.

"Late in the afternoon," writes Dr. Stanley, "we reached Bethany. I then took my place close beside the Prince. Every one else fell back by design or accident, and at the head of the cavalcade we moved on towards the famous view. This was the one half-hour which, throughout the journey, I had determined to have alone with the Prince, and I succeeded."

During Dr. Stanley's previous journey to the Holy Land he had not been permitted to visit the closely-guarded cave of Machpelah, but on this occasion, thanks to the diplomacy of General Bruce, not only the Prince of Wales, but also his chaplain, was allowed to set foot within the sacred precincts. Even to Royal personages the Mosque of Hebron had remained absolutely barred for nearly seven hundred years, and on the present occasion the Turkish official in charge declared that "for no one but for the eldest son of the

Queen of England would he have allowed the gate to be opened; indeed, the Princes of any other nation should have passed over his body before doing so."

His Royal Highness, with his usual thoughtfulness, had made Dr. Stanley's entrance with himself a condition of his going in at all, and when the latter went up to the Prince to thank him and to say that but for him he would never have had this great opportunity, the young man answered with touching and almost reproachful simplicity, "High station, you see, sir, has, after all, some merits, some advantages." "Yes, sir," replied Dr. Stanley, "and I hope that you will always make as good a use of it."

On the party's return to Jerusalem, they witnessed the Samaritan Passover, and Easter Sunday, 20th April, was spent by the shores of Lake Tiberias.

During the journey from Tiberias to Damascus the Prince and his escort lived in tents, an experience which His Royal Highness seems to have thoroughly enjoyed. From Damascus the party turned westward, reaching Beyrout on 6th May, and after visiting Tyre and Sidon they proceeded to Tripoli. On 13th May His Royal Highness left the shores of Syria, visiting on his homeward journey Patmos, Ephesus, Smyrna, Constantinople, Athens, and Malta.

It was very characteristic of the Prince that wherever he went he collected a number of flowers or leaves from every famous spot, which, after having been carefully dried by him, were sent to his sister, the Princess Royal.

It was very soon after his return from the East that the Prince of Wales played for the first time an important part in a family gathering—the wedding of his favourite sister, Princess Alice, to Prince Louis of Hesse. The bride was given away by her uncle, the Duke of Saxe-Coburg-Gotha, but the young Prince of Wales acted as master of the house during the quiet week which preceded the ceremony.

CHAPTER IV

THE PRINCE OF WALES'S MARRIAGE

As is very generally known, the marriage of the Prince of Wales to Princess Alexandra of Denmark was brought about in quite a romantic fashion. It is said that long before His Royal Highness saw his future wife he was very much attracted by a glimpse of her photograph, shown him by one of his friends. Be that as it may, it is certain that though many Princesses had been spoken of in connection with the Prince, and at one time there were actually negotiations impending with the view of his engagement to the daughter of a German Royal House, all such schemes were instantly abandoned after he had seen the beautiful Danish Princess.

The first informal meeting took place in the Cathedral of Worms during the Prince's foreign tour in 1861. The Prince, accompanied by his tutor and equerry, had gone to examine the frescoes, and when wandering through the beautiful old Cathedral they met Prince Christian of Denmark and his daughter intent on the same object. Somewhat later His Royal Highness again met his future wife when he was staying with his sister, the Crown Princess of Prussia, at Heidelberg, and the Prince Consort puts on record in his diary that "the young people seem to have taken a warm liking for each other."

Later, after the Prince Consort's death, during a short visit which he paid to his cousin, the King of the Belgians, the Prince again met Princess Alexandra, and it is said that King Leopold had a considerable share in arranging the preliminaries of the marriage, for it was while the Prince and Princess were both staying at Laeken that the Queen's formal consent to her son's making a Danish alliance was granted.

THE PRINCE OF WALES'S MARRIAGE 43

The formal betrothal took place on 9th September 1862, but even then what had occurred was only known to a comparatively small circle of friends and relations, for it was not till the eve of His Royal Highness's coming of age that his engagement was formally

THE PRINCESS ALEXANDRA OF DENMARK

From a Photograph in the possession of the King of Denmark, taken on 1st December 1862

announced in the *London Gazette* and so made known to the whole British Empire.

The announcement roused the greatest enthusiasm, for deep as had been the public sympathy with Her Majesty, a widowed Court could not but cast a very real gloom, not only over society, but over all those directly and indirectly interested in the sumptuary trades and the wide distribution of wealth. It was universally felt that the marriage of the Heir-Apparent would inaugurate a new era of prosperity, and scarce a dissenting voice was raised at the very liberal grant voted by the House of Commons for the Royal couple.

On the proposal of Lord Palmerston, it was decided that the Prince of Wales should receive from the country an income of £40,000 a year, with an added £10,000 a year to be specially set apart for the Princess. And so it came to pass that the Heir-Apparent and his bride began housekeeping with an income of somewhat over £100,000 a year, for, owing to the Prince Consort's foresight and good sense, out of the savings made during his son's long minority, Sandringham, of which the initial cost was £220,000, had been purchased.

Unlike most Royal engagements, that of the Prince and Princess of Wales lasted nearly six months, but active preparations for the wedding did not begin till the official announcement had been made.

Although Princess Alexandra had visited England as a child in order to make the acquaintance of her great-aunt, the Duchess of Cambridge, it was at Laeken that she was presented to her future mother-in-law, Queen Victoria, who was then paying a visit *incognito* to King Leopold. Later on, the young Princess, accompanied by her father, paid the Queen an informal visit at Osborne. She did not on this occasion come to London or take part in any public function, but rumours of her beauty and of her charm of manner had become rife, and as the wedding day, which had been fixed for 10th March, approached, the public interest and excitement were strung to the highest pitch. It was felt that Denmark's loss was Britain's gain, and Alfred Tennyson, the Poet Laureate, voiced most happily the universal feeling in his fine lines :

> Clash, ye bells, in the merry March air!
> Flash, ye cities, in rivers of fire!
> And welcome her, welcome the land's desire,
>   Alexandra.

Even the humblest of Her Majesty's subjects usually finds a good deal to do during the weeks that precede his marriage, and it will

THE PRINCE OF WALES'S MARRIAGE 45

be easily understood that the high station of the Prince of Wales rather augmented than diminished these engrossing occupations.

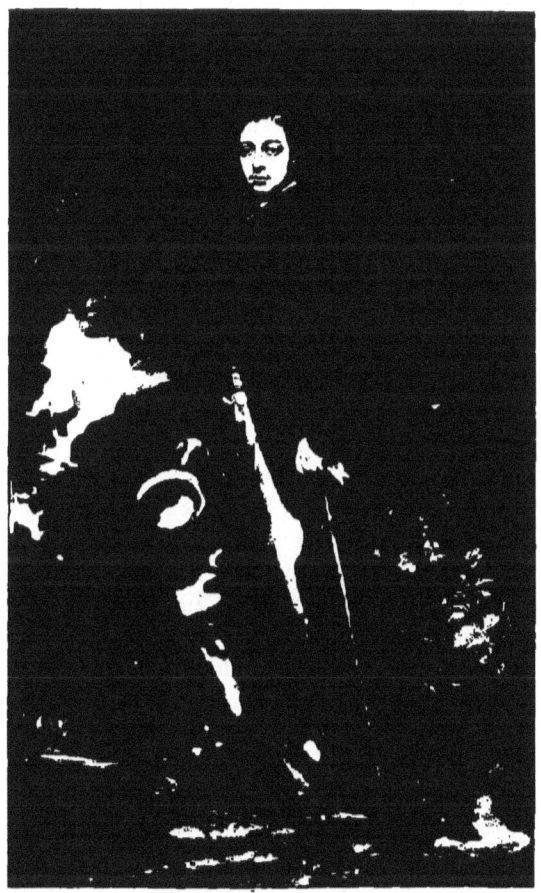

THE PRINCE ON COMING OF AGE
From an Engraving published by Henry Graves and Co.

He had to receive and suitably acknowledge countless addresses of congratulation from individuals, corporations, and other public bodies; he had to superintend the extensive alterations which were still being carried out at Marlborough House; he had to pass in review the innumerable details of the various elaborate functions which were to mark the occasion of his marriage; and last but not least it was considered desirable that he should now go through the somewhat trying ceremony of taking his seat in the House of Lords.

Nearly three-quarters of a century had elapsed since the Heir-Apparent to the British Crown had taken the oath and his seat as a Peer of the Realm. It was on 5th February 1863, within a few weeks of his marriage, that the Prince of Wales went through this historic ceremony, and it is a curious fact that the business before the House of Lords on that occasion was an Address from the Crown to the British Parliament announcing the Prince's approaching marriage. It is also noteworthy that soon after the ceremony the two chief dignitaries of the English Church, the new Archbishops of Canterbury and York, also took the oaths and their seats upon the Episcopal benches of the House.

The Duchess of Cambridge and Princess Mary and a brilliant array of Peeresses and ladies from the various foreign Embassies and Legations were present at the ceremony, which was invested with a great deal of pomp and solemnity. After prayers had been read by the Bishop of Worcester, a procession emerged from the Prince's Chamber, and advanced slowly up the floor of the House. First came the Usher of the Black Rod, followed immediately by the Garter King at Arms, attired in his robes. Then came the Prince of Wales, preceded by an equerry, bearing his coronet on an embroidered crimson cushion. His Royal Highness was also accompanied by the Duke of Cambridge, the Duke of Argyll, the Hereditary Grand Chamberlain, and Lord Edward Howard, who represented the infant Duke of Norfolk, Hereditary Earl Marshal.

The Prince of Wales wore the scarlet and ermine robes of a Duke over the uniform of a General. He also wore the Order of the Garter, the Order of the Golden Fleece, and the Order of the Star of India. As he entered the House, the Peers rose in a body, the Lord Chancellor alone remaining seated and covered with his official hat. His Royal Highness then advanced to the Woolsack, and placed his patent of peerage and writ of summons in the hands

THE PRINCE OF WALES'S MARRIAGE 47

of the Chancellor. The oaths were administered to him at the table by the Clerk of Parliament, the titles under which the Prince was sworn being those of Duke of Cornwall, Earl of Chester, Earl of Carrick, Earl of Rothesay, and Lord of the Isles.

After the roll had been signed the procession moved on, and His Royal Highness, on reaching the right-hand side of the Throne,

THE PRINCESS IN 1863
From the Painting by Madame Jerichau, published by Henry Graves and Co.

took his seat upon the Chair of State specially appropriated on State occasions to the Prince of Wales. While thus seated he placed on his head the cocked hat worn by general officers in full dress. The Prince and the other Peers finally left the House, retiring by the entrance at the right of the Throne in the same order as they had entered.

About an hour later His Royal Highness re-entered the House dressed in ordinary afternoon costume, and took his seat on one of the cross-benches, thereby formally dissociating himself from either political party. The Prince remained almost throughout the entire debate. When leaving he shook hands with the Earl of Derby and a number of other Peers whom he recognised.

As is well known, the only votes which the Prince has ever given in the House of Lords have been in favour of the Bill for legalising marriage with a deceased wife's sister, but he is a constant visitor at the Houses of Parliament when anything of special interest is going on, and there is no doubt that he takes the keenest interest in the political questions of the day.

The Danish people were extremely pleased at the marriage their Princess was making, and so determined were they that she should not go dowerless, that 100,000 kroner, known as "the People's Dowry," were presented to her, and countless presents, many of them of the humblest description, poured in upon her from all over the sea-girt kingdom. By the Princess's own wish, 3000 thalers were distributed among six Danish brides belonging to the poorer classes during the year of Her Royal Highness's marriage. The fact became known, and naturally greatly added to Her Royal Highness's popularity, and from the day she left Copenhagen to that on which she landed on British soil, the journey of Prince Christian and his family, for Princess Alexandra was accompanied by her father and mother, and brothers and sisters, was nothing short of a triumphal progress.

The Royal *cortège* left Denmark on 26th February, reaching Cologne on 2nd March. There the Prince of Wales's *fiancée* received the first greetings of her future husband's people, the British residents. The whole party were also royally entertained at Brussels by the Court of Flanders; and at Flushing they found a squadron of British men-of-war to escort the Royal yacht *Victoria and Albert*.

On the morning of 7th March the Danish Royal Family first saw the white cliffs of Old England, and at twenty minutes past eleven, the Royal yacht, which had steamed slowly up the river amid craft splendidly decorated with flags and flowers, anchored opposite the pier at Gravesend. A moment later the Prince of Wales, accompanied by a numerous suite, and attired in a blue frock-coat and

THE PRINCE OF WALES'S MARRIAGE

gray trousers, stepped on board. As His Royal Highness reached the deck Princess Alexandra advanced to the door of the State cabin to meet him, and, to the great delight of the assembled crowds ashore and afloat, the Prince, walking quickly towards his bride, took her by the hand and kissed her most affectionately.

THE PRINCESS
From a Photograph by Mayall in 1863

Then followed the procession through London; every street, from the humblest portions of the East End to the great West End thoroughfares, was lavishly decorated, and the Prince and Princess accepted addresses presented by the Corporation and many other London public bodies.

The Princess of Wales gave some special sittings for a medal which was struck to commemorate her public entry into the City of London, and it remains one of the finest examples of Wyon's art. The reverse represents the Princess Alexandra, led by the Prince of Wales, and attended by Hymen, being welcomed by the City of London, who is accompanied by Peace and Plenty, the latter carrying the diamond necklace and earrings which the City offered to the Princess as a wedding present. In the background is the triumphal arch erected by the Corporation at London Bridge, where Her Royal Highness first entered the City precincts. The medals were struck only in bronze, and were presented to the Queen, the Prince and Princess of Wales, all the members of the Royal family, the Royal and distinguished guests who were asked to the wedding, and the members of the Corporation of the City of London.

The poor young Princess must have been glad when that long day came to an end, for the Royal train from Paddington to Windsor did not start till a quarter past five, and thus from early morning till late in the afternoon our future Queen had been compelled to remain the cynosure of all eyes. It is an interesting fact that the engine which took the Princess to Windsor was driven by the Earl of Caithness, then the best known amateur locomotive engineer of the day.

As may easily be imagined, the Royal borough was determined not to be outdone by London in the matter of a bridal welcome. The Eton boys presented an address signed by the whole 800; and then came the arrival at the Castle, where the Queen, surrounded by all her children and a large number of Royal visitors, received her future daughter-in-law. Then followed two days of almost complete rest for the Princess.

The Prince, in addition to the multifarious duties which beset even humble individuals when they are about to enter the holy estate, was also compelled to hold his first *levée* within a few days of his wedding. Over a thousand gentlemen had the honour of being presented to His Royal Highness, the presentations, by Her Majesty's pleasure, being considered as equal to presentations to the Queen. The *levée*, which was held in St. James's Palace, was also attended by about seventeen hundred of the nobility and gentry, all

THE MARRIAGE OF THE PRINCE AND PRINCESS
From a Painting by W. P. Frith, R.A., published by Henry Graves and Co.

anxious to do honour to the Heir-Apparent, who was, it need hardly be added, attended by a brilliant Court.

The Prince of Wales and the British Royal Family had not been idle during the period of the engagement. His Royal Highness himself ordered and examined the designs for all the gifts about to be presented by him to his bride, and to her family whom he specially wished to honour. His first present to her, the engagement ring, has since served as keeper for the Princess's wedding ring. It is a very beautiful example of the jeweller's art, being set with six precious stones—a beryl, an emerald, a ruby, a turquoise, a jacinth, and a second emerald, the initials of the six gems spelling the Prince's family name, "Bertie." His Royal Highness's gifts also included a complete set of diamonds and pearls, comprising diadem, necklace, stomacher, and bracelet ; also a very beautiful waist-clasp, formed of two large turquoises inlaid with Arabic characters, and mounted in gold.

Her Majesty presented her future daughter-in-law with a set of opals and diamonds exactly similar in form to that designed for Princess Alice by the Prince Consort. The Queen also gave the Prince of Wales a centre-piece, which was presented to him in the name of the Prince Consort and of herself. This fine piece of work had also been designed by the Prince Consort as a gift to his son. It has a group at the base showing Edward I. presenting his heir to the Welsh chieftains, and round the base are portraits of six Princes of Wales. Her Majesty, whose thoughtful care was shown in this as in many other matters, also gave the Prince of Wales and his bride a great deal of valuable plate.

The London jewellers had certainly cause for rejoicing over the Royal marriage, for the Prince, not content with presenting his bride-elect with a number of other very costly gifts, also showered gems on all his own and her relations. Neither were his friends forgotten. He ordered twenty breast-pins, heart-shaped, encircled by brilliants, with the initials of himself and the Princess traced in rubies, diamonds, and emeralds occupying the centre of each heart. These were distributed to his brothers and to a number of his intimates. To his future mother-in-law, Princess Christian of Denmark, the Prince gave a beautiful bracelet, containing a miniature

THE PRINCE OF WALES'S MARRIAGE 53

of himself; also a diamond, ruby, and emerald brooch, inscribed with the date of the marriage, and containing miniature portraits of

A Contemporary Design for the Marriage
of the Prince and Princess

himself and the Princess. An exactly similar jewel was presented by Princess Alexandra to the Queen.

In order efficiently to conduct the Royal wedding in St. George's Chapel at Windsor, it became necessary to build proper apartments for the accommodation of the bride and bridegroom on their arrival, and for the Lord Chamberlain to marshal the processions without any danger of a hitch. With this object the Board of Works built an immense Gothic hall, opening out of the west door of the Chapel, and surrounded by apartments appropriated to the use of the Royal Family. Facing the Chapel, the two rooms upon the right were assigned to the bridegroom, and those on the left to the bride.

The marriage of the Prince and Princess of Wales was the first Royal marriage which had been celebrated in St. George's Chapel since that of Henry I. in 1122. The day was kept as a public holiday throughout the country, and the attention of the whole kingdom was concentrated on Windsor. The ceremony took place on 10th March 1863, at 12 o'clock. The total number of persons admitted to the chapel did not exceed 900 ladies and gentlemen, exclusive of the Guards and of the attendants on duty.

The scene will never be forgotten by those who had the privilege of being present. It was an extraordinarily magnificent pageant, heralds and trumpeters in coats of cloth of gold adding greatly to the brilliancy and pomp. No touch of mourning was allowed to mar the brightness of the occasion.

The Queen surveyed the scene from the Royal closet, which, placed on the north side of the Communion Table, is really a small room in the body of the Castle with a window opening into the Chapel. Her Majesty was clad in deep black, even to her gloves, and she wore a close-fitting widow's cap, but in deference to the occasion she had consented to put on the broad blue ribbon of the Order of the Garter with the glittering star, and this was specially noticed by the few persons who, from the body of the Chapel, caught a glimpse of their beloved Sovereign.

The bridegroom, as in duty bound, arrived some time before the bride. He was supported by his uncle, the Duke of Saxe-Coburg, and his brother-in-law, the Crown Prince of Prussia, and wore the uniform of a British General, the Collar of the Garter, the Order of the Star of India, and the rich flowing purple velvet mantle of a Knight of the Garter. His supporters also wore the robes of the Garter, and the three were naturally the observed of all observers till the arrival of the bride, who came in upon the stroke of half-past twelve.

THE PRINCE OF WALES'S MARRIAGE 55

Princess Alexandra, who was given away by her father, wore, according to the notions of that day, a very beautiful and splendid wedding dress. It consisted of a white satin skirt, trimmed with garlands of orange blossom and puffings of tulle and Honiton lace, the bodice being draped with the same lace, while the train of silver moire antique was covered with nosegays of orange blossom and puffings of tulle. In addition to the necklace, earrings, and brooch presented to Her Royal Highness by the bridegroom, she wore the *rivière* of diamonds given by the Corporation of London, and three bracelets, presented to her respectively by the Queen, the ladies of Leeds, and the ladies of Manchester. On her beautiful hair, which was very simply dressed, lay a wreath of orange blossoms covered by a veil of Honiton lace.

The bridal bouquet was composed of orange blossoms, white rosebuds, orchids, and sprigs of myrtle, the latter being taken from the same bush as that from which the myrtle used in the Princess Royal's bridal bouquet was cut.

As the Princess moved slowly up the Chapel her train was carried by eight bridesmaids, Lady Victoria Scott, Lady Victoria Howard, Lady Agneta Yorke, Lady Feodora Wellesley, Lady Diana Beauclerk, Lady Georgina Hamilton, Lady Alma Bruce, and Lady Helena Hare. They each wore dresses of white tulle over white glacé silk, trimmed with blush roses, shamrocks, and white heather, with wreaths to correspond, and each also wore a locket presented to her by the Prince of Wales, composed of coral and diamonds, signifying the red and white which are the colours of Denmark, while in the centre of each was a crystal cipher forming the letters "A. E. A." twined together in a monogram designed by Princess Alice.

It is an interesting fact that all these ladies are still living, and many of them have since become the Princess's personal friends. Even now she occasionally wears the splendid diamond and enamelled bracelet, made in eight compartments, each containing a miniature of one of the Royal bridesmaids, which was their gift to her on the occasion of the marriage.

The ceremony itself did not last very long. The Prince is recorded to have answered his "I will" right manfully, but the

Princess's answers were almost inaudible. As soon as the Prince of Wales and the Princess Alexandra were man and wife, they turned to the congregation hand in hand, bowing low to the Queen, who, in returning the salutation, made a gesture of blessing rather than of ceremonious acknowledgment.

Dr. Norman Macleod wrote: "I returned home and went back to the marriage on the 10th of March. . . . I got behind Kingsley, Stanley, Birch, and in a famous place, being in front of the Royal pair. We saw better than any except the clergy. It was a gorgeous sight, yet somehow did not excite me. I suppose I am past this.

"Two things struck me much. One was the whole of the Royal Princesses weeping, though concealing their tears with their bouquets, as they saw their brother, who was to them but their 'Bertie,' and their dead father's son, standing alone waiting for his bride. The other was the Queen's expression as she raised her eyes to Heaven, while her husband's Chorale was sung. She seemed to be with him alone before the throne of God."

Mr. W. P. Frith, who had been commissioned to execute a painting of the Royal marriage for the Queen, was accommodated with a special corner for himself and his sketch-book, and later, all those who had taken part in the historic pageant sat to him for portraits with the most excellent result.

On their return to the Castle a few moments later the bride and bridegroom were met by the Queen and conducted to the Green Drawing-Room, where the formal attestation of the marriage took place.

It may be added that among those present at the marriage and afterwards at the wedding breakfast were the Rev. H. M. Birch and the Rev. C. F. Tarver, the Prince's tutors, and when lunch was over these gentlemen were informed that their old pupil sent them a souvenir of himself, of which he desired their acceptance. This souvenir proved to be in each case a copy of the Holy Scriptures, handsomely bound, and containing an inscription in His Royal Highness's own handwriting.

The wedding breakfast, which was served in St. George's Hall, was very sumptuous, but out of respect to the Queen's recent bereavement there were very few speeches—a circumstance which probably did not greatly disappoint either the bride or the bridegroom. While the marriage was actually in progress the King of

On the Wedding Day
From a Photograph by Mayall

Denmark was entertaining both the rich and poor in his kingdom right royally, and it must have been a pleasant thought for the Princess to know that her marriage was filling with gladness innumerable multitudes both of her own people and of her husband's future subjects.

At four o'clock the Prince and Princess of Wales took their departure for Osborne, where a very short honeymoon was spent. On their return home, which in this case meant Windsor, it was noticed that the lovely bride looked the very picture of happiness. The streets of Windsor were decorated with flags, and the Royal borough looked as gay as it did on the wedding day.

After the marriage of the Prince of Wales the Liturgy of the Church of England was officially altered by the introduction of the name of the Princess of Wales into the Prayer for the Royal Family. The Scottish Church was also officially instructed to pray for " Her Most Sacred Majesty Queen Victoria, Albert Edward Prince of Wales, the Princess of Wales, and all the Royal Family."

CHAPTER V

EARLY MARRIED LIFE

AMONG the very first visitors entertained at Sandringham by the Royal bride and bridegroom was Dr. Stanley, who spent Easter Sunday with them there.

"On the evening of Easter Eve," he writes, "the Princess came to me in a corner of the drawing-room with her Prayer Book, and I went through the Communion Service with her, explaining the peculiarities and the likenesses and differences to and from the Danish Service. She was most simple and fascinating. . . . My visit to Sandringham gave me intense pleasure. I was there for three days. I read the whole Service, preached, then gave the first English Sacrament to this 'angel in the Palace.' I saw a great deal of her, and can truly say that she is as charming and beautiful a creature as ever passed through a fairy tale."

One of the first public appearances made by the Prince of Wales after his marriage was at the Royal Academy dinner, where he made an excellent short speech, greatly impressing those who were present by his modesty and good sense. William Makepeace Thackeray was among the speakers on this occasion, which was very shortly before the famous novelist's lamented death. At the anniversary of the Royal Literary Fund some months later the Prince made some graceful and appropriate allusions to the great writer whom the Empire had lost. He spoke with evident feeling of the fact that Thackeray had been the life of the Fund, always ready to open his purse for the relief of literary men struggling with pecuniary difficulties.

This spring was a very busy time for both their Royal Highnesses.

On 8th June the Prince and Princess were sumptuously entertained by the Lord Mayor at the Guildhall, when the Prince of Wales took up the freedom of the City, to which he was entitled by patrimony. The entertainments included a great ball, which the Princess of Wales opened, dancing a quadrille with the Lord Mayor, while the Prince had the Lady Mayoress for his partner.

A week later the Royal couple attended "Commem." at Oxford. They received a splendid welcome both from the University authorities and the undergraduates. The honorary degree of Doctor of Civil Law was conferred on the Prince in the Sheldonian Theatre, where the wildest uproar prevailed, till amid a sudden lull of perfect silence the Princess entered with Dr. Liddell, then Dean of Christ Church. Scarcely had she traversed half the distance to her seat when a cheer loud and deep arose, and seemed to shake the theatre to its foundation, to the evident satisfaction of the Prince.

After the ceremony was over their Royal Highnesses escaped from all their friends and entertainers and took the opportunity of going over what had been the Prince's rooms as an undergraduate. That same evening a ball was given in the Prince's honour in the Corn Exchange by the Apollo Lodge of Freemasons.

Shortly after their visit to Oxford the Prince and Princess celebrated their house-warming at Marlborough House by an evening party and a ball. During the summer months the Prince and Princess spent some time at Sandringham in the original house, which at that time stood in an isolated park, and which has now been replaced by the present very much larger and more comfortable mansion. There can be no doubt that the Princess's strong affection for her country home is based on the tender recollections of her early married life. It is a significant fact that when the new Sandringham House was built Her Royal Highness begged that her boudoir in the new mansion might be arranged so as to be an exact reproduction of her boudoir in the old house.

The only public function at which the Prince of Wales was present during 1863 occurred in August, when he visited Halifax and opened a new town hall there.

Much satisfaction was felt when the news became known that

EARLY MARRIED LIFE 61

the Queen hoped to welcome the first of her British grandchildren in the month of March. One Friday evening, early in January, shortly

THE PRINCESS IN 1863
From the Painting by Lauchert, published by Colnaghi

after the Princess, who was staying, had been skating on Virginia Water, near Windsor, her eldest child appeared so unexpectedly that for a while the Royal baby had to be wrapped in cotton wool, for all the beautiful layette which was in course of preparation was at Marlborough House.

The rejoicings over the event, both in this country and in Denmark, were naturally very great, more especially when it became known that the Royal infant was none the worse for his early arrival. Among the two Royal families most immediately concerned the interest and excitement was intense. Princess Alice wrote to the Queen on 9th January 1894, " I was aghast on receiving Bertie's telegram this morning announcing the birth of their little son." But this feeling of trepidation quickly gave place to one of relief when the bulletins announced the steady progress of both mother and babe, and soon the British public saw many charming photographs and portraits of the Princess of Wales in her new *rôle* of mother. At the time of the birth of the Duke of Clarence the Princess was not yet twenty, but, like the Queen, she seems to have been wholly absorbed in her maternal duties, and at any moment she would joyfully give up attending a State function or ball in order to spend an hour in her nursery.

It need hardly be said that the first portion of the Prince and Princess of Wales's married life was overshadowed by the war between Denmark and Prussia. The young Princess was naturally strongly patriotic in her sympathies. At breakfast one morning a foolish equerry read out a telegram which announced a success of the Austro-Prussian forces, whereupon Her Royal Highness burst into tears, and the Prince, it is said, thoroughly lost his temper for once, and rated his equerry as soundly as his ancestor, Henry VIII., might have done. An amusing story went the round of the clubs about this time. It was said that a Royal visitor at Windsor asked Princess Beatrice what she would like for a present. The child stood in doubt, and begged the Princess of Wales to advise her. The result of a whispered conversation between the two was that the little Princess declared aloud that she would like to have Bismarck's head on a charger!

In July 1864 the Prince laid the foundation-stone of the new West Wing of the London Hospital. He was accompanied by the Princess. This was one of the first occasions on which he showed his great interest in hospital management. The fact that there was a separate ward for the Jews aroused his keen interest. In the same

THE PRINCESS IN 1864

From the Painting by Lauchert, published by Henry Graves and Co.

month the Prince and Princess went to the Fourth of June at Eton, and also stayed at Goodwood for the races. In the middle of August they went to the Highlands, visiting Stirling Castle on the way. They spent some weeks at Abergeldie, entertaining a great deal. Dr. Norman Macleod stayed with them there. It was during this stay in Scotland that the Prince and Princess of Wales first became intimate with the family of their future son-in-law, and the Countess of Fife, his mother, gave a great picnic in their honour.

That autumn they went from Dundee to Denmark, being accompanied by their baby, now nearly a year old. This was the Prince's first visit to his wife's home. They received a most enthusiastic welcome, and were splendidly entertained. At Bernsdorf, where the Royal party spent several days, a number of shooting parties were organised in honour of His Royal Highness, who, certainly for the first time in his life, was invited to shoot foxes. He bagged two, and some of the teeth of the animals were set as breast-pins for him.

From Elsinore the Prince and Princess went in their yacht to Stockholm in order to pay a visit to the King and Queen of Sweden. In Sweden also the Prince was invited to take part in several hunting expeditions. One odd bag resulted in ten foxes, six hares, and seventeen stags.

After sending Prince Albert Victor home with Countess de Grey, the Royal couple travelled back *via* Germany and Belgium, visiting on the way Prince and Princess Louis of Hesse, at Darmstadt; and making a short stay at Brussels. Then they came home for the rest of the autumn to Sandringham, where the Princess spent her twentieth birthday.

The year 1865 proved an eventful one both to the Prince and the Princess. The Prince paid his first State visit to Ireland, opening the International Exhibition of Dublin on 9th May, and a little less than a month later Prince George of Wales was born at Marlborough House.

Although, however, there have at various times been more or less serious fires in the Royal palaces, Sandringham, for instance, having been almost destroyed by a conflagration within the last few years, His Royal Highness has only once been really in a fire, and this was just a month after his second son's birth. The fire began

EARLY MARRIED LIFE

in the floor then styled the nursery floor, and after the Princess of Wales had been moved to another part of the house with her two

THE PRINCESS WITH THE BABY PRINCE ALBERT VICTOR
Photograph in 1864 by Vernon Heath, published by McQueen

children, the Prince set to work with the utmost energy to check the flames. It need hardly be said that very soon the whole of

London seemed to be congregated in Pall Mall and St. James's Park. At first it could not be made out where the fire was coming from, and the Prince helped to rip up the whole of the nursery floor before the mischief could be traced, and while doing so he nearly had a bad accident, for he fell some distance through the rafters.

At last, however, the fire was got under and it was found that comparatively little harm had been done. Then for the first time it occurred to some one to ask if Marlborough House was insured. Strangely enough this very important precaution had not been taken. Now, however, both the Prince's town and country houses are insured to their full value.

The Prince of Wales from childhood has always shown the keenest interest in firemen and fires. During many years of his life he used to be informed whenever a really big blaze was signalled, and he has attended *incognito* most of the great London fires during the last thirty years.

About this time the Prince of Wales visited the gigantic steamship *Great Eastern*, off Sheerness, in order to see the Atlantic telegraph cable, which had just been completed. His Royal Highness was received by a number of prominent engineers, and while he was present the last section of the cable was being wound into the tanks on board the *Great Eastern* from the vessel alongside which had brought it from the works at Greenwich. A message was sent through one of the coils, the length of which was equivalent to the distance from Sheerness to Valentia. The signals transmitted, "God Save the Queen," were received at the other end of the coil in the course of a few seconds, a fact which, commonplace as it may now seem, struck the onlookers in the year 1865 with amazement. The Prince visited every portion of the huge ship, and accepted specimen pieces of portions of the cable in various stages of manufacture.

In that same year, that is two years after her marriage, the Princess of Wales performed her first public act by opening the Cambridge School of Art. It was in 1865 also that the Prince attended his first public dinner as President of the Royal Literary Fund, and it was on this occasion that His Royal Highness toasted the ladies in these graceful words:—" In the presence of a society accustomed

EARLY MARRIED LIFE 67

to cultivating with such success the flowers of literature, it would be unpardonable to forget the flowers of society."

THE PRINCE, THE PRINCESS, AND PRINCE ALBERT VICTOR
Photograph in 1864 by Vernon Heath, published by McQueen

During that summer the Prince and Princess of Wales visited Cornwall, and went down the Botallack tin mine, near St. Just, the depth of which is about 200 fathoms. The bottom level of the mine extends horizontally about half a mile beneath the sea. A part of this mine belongs to His Royal Highness as Duke of Cornwall. During the same tour the Prince visited Land's End. The day was exceptionally clear and fine, and His Royal Highness lingered for some time among the grim rocks which form the westernmost point of England.

All this time the Queen was living in the strictest retirement, and the great shadow of the Prince Consort's death had thrown scarcely less gloom over the life of his eldest son. The Prince of Wales mourned deeply for his father, and it is significant that he never lost an opportunity of testifying in his public speeches to the high purpose and noble aims which had distinguished Prince Albert's life. To the cost of the mausoleum at Frogmore the Prince of Wales contributed from his private purse no less a sum than £10,000. At the end of 1865 the Prince sustained another severe blow in the death of Lord Palmerston, whom he had honoured with his special friendship and whom he had been accustomed to consult in his private affairs.

Not till February 1866 did the Queen consent to open Parliament again in person. She was accompanied by the Prince of Wales and two of her daughters, the Princess of Wales being accommodated with a seat on the Woolsack facing the Throne.

It was in this year, when the Austro-German war was going on, that the Prince established special telegraphic communication between Marlborough House and the seat of war. Like the Queen, he is a shrewd observer of foreign politics, and when he is called upon to reign, will probably be the best unofficial Foreign Minister in the country. His Royal Highness has since kept up in every important war the practice of securing the earliest possible telegraphic information, notably in the Franco-Prussian, the Russo-Turkish, and the Greco-Turkish wars.

In the summer of 1866 the Prince of Wales laid the foundation-stone of the new building of the British and Foreign Bible Society. The Earl of Shaftesbury, President of the Society, the Lord Mayor, the Archbishop of York, and the Bishop of Winchester received the Prince.

EARLY MARRIED LIFE

In his speech His Royal Highness recalled the fact that only sixty-three years previously Mr. Wilberforce had met with a few friends in a small room in a dingy counting-house and had established the Bible Society, while at the time that he, the Prince, was speaking, the Society had already spent six millions of money in the furtherance of its objects, and that it had contributed to the translation of the Bible into two hundred and eighty different languages and dialects. The Prince further said :

"I have an hereditary claim to be here on this occasion. My grandfather, the Duke of Kent, warmly advocated the claims of the Society, and it is gratifying to me to reflect that the two modern versions of the Scriptures more widely circulated than any others—the German and English —were both in their origin connected with my family. The translation of Martin Luther was executed under the protection of the Elector of Saxony, the collateral ancestor of my lamented father ; whilst that of William Tyndale—the foundation of the present Authorised English Version—was introduced with the sanction of the Royal predecessor of my mother, the Queen who first desired that 'the Bible shall have free course through all Christendom, but especially in my own realm.' It is my hope and trust that, under the Divine guidance, the wider diffusion and a deeper study of the Scriptures will, in this as in every age, be at once the surest guarantee of the progress and liberty of mind, and the means of multiplying in the present form the consolations of our holy religion."

THE QUEEN WITH PRINCE ALBERT VICTOR

Photograph by Hughes and Mullins, Ryde

In the autumn following, the Prince and Princess, accompanied by their two sons, visited the Duke and Duchess of Sutherland at Dunrobin. At that time the most northern point of railway communication was at Ardgay, and thence the Prince and Princess had to drive a distance of twenty-five miles before they could reach Dunrobin Castle. All along the route they received a most enthusiastic welcome. They arrived at night at the Castle and were received in Royal Highland style. Among those asked to meet them were the Duke of Edinburgh, the Prince of Saxe-Weimar, and many members of the leading Scotch nobility. The Prince of Wales reviewed the Sutherland Volunteers in the grounds of the Castle, and later, on the same day, the Duke of Sutherland announced that it was the Prince's wish that the whole of the corps should adopt the kilt as their uniform, His Royal Highness having a preference for the national costume.

Shortly after their return from Scotland the Prince and Princess of Wales had the pleasure of entertaining the Queen of Denmark and her two younger children, and they spent some time at Sandringham with the Princess of Wales, while the Prince went to Russia in order to be present at the marriage of his sister-in-law, Princess Dagmar, to the then Cesarewitch. It was quite late in the year and it was considered that the cold in St. Petersburg would be too severe for the Princess to accompany her husband. The Prince, who attended the Imperial marriage in his official capacity, was accompanied by a considerable suite, including Lord Frederick Paulet, Viscount Hamilton, the Marquis of Blandford, and Major Teesdale. On His Royal Highness's arrival at St. Petersburg he was met at the railway terminus by the Emperor of Russia, the Cesarewitch, and the Grand Dukes; and he was given splendid quarters at the Hermitage Palace.

The Prince of Wales has always been known to have a great liking for Russia and the Russian people, and he is himself very popular in St. Petersburg. After the Imperial marriage he visited Moscow, being accompanied by the Crown Prince of Denmark. The Princes went over the Kremlin; and the Prince of Wales paid a call on the Metropolitan Archbishop, the highest dignitary of the Russian Church. The aged ecclesiastic received His Royal Highness in a perfectly plain cell. They conversed for a quarter of an hour, and as the Prince was leaving, the Metropolitan gave him his blessing, and with the assistance of his monks accompanied his Royal visitor to the door.

CHAPTER VI

ILLNESS OF THE PRINCESS—ROYAL VISIT TO IRELAND—
CONTINENTAL AND EASTERN TOUR

THE year 1867 was, if not very eventful, an anxious one for the Prince and Princess of Wales, for both before and after the birth of their third child, now the Duchess of Fife, on 20th February, the Princess suffered from acute rheumatism and inflammation of a knee-joint. Her illness caused so much anxiety at the Danish Court that her father and mother came over and spent some time in London. The Prince was most devoted in his attentions to the invalid, and actually had his bureau moved into her sick-room in order that he might not be separated from her in her convalescence even by the imperious demands of his enormous correspondence. Happily Her Royal Highness grew quite strong again, but the serious nature of her illness may be judged from the fact that she was not able to drive out until 9th July. Naturally for the rest of that year the Prince and Princess lived very quietly and went about as little as possible.

Five years after their marriage the Prince and Princess of Wales paid a visit to Ireland, and their reception was marked by a very genuine demonstration of cordiality and even of enthusiasm. On arriving in Kingstown Harbour Her Royal Highness was presented, as the Queen had been in 1849, with a white dove, emblematic of the affection and goodwill which she was supposed to be bringing to the distressful country. The Prince, with his usual tact, declared it to be his wish that no troops should be present in the streets of Dublin. Entire reliance was accordingly placed on the loyalty and hospitable spirit of the people, and, in spite of many doleful prognostications to the contrary, the Royal visit was successful from every point of view.

It has often been asserted that the Prince of Wales is fonder of the Emerald Isle than is any other member of his family; he certainly numbers several Irishmen among his closest friends. Although His Royal Highness thoroughly enjoyed his visit, this one week in 1868 was one of the most tiring ever spent by the Prince. Like his younger son, the Duke of York, twenty-nine years later, the Prince was installed with great pomp as a Knight of the Order of St. Patrick, on which occasion he used the sword worn by George IV. The Prince also unveiled with much ceremony a statue of Edmund Burke. The *Times* described the exertions which the Prince went through in the following passage :—

"There were presentations and receptions, and receiving and answering addresses, processions, walking, riding and driving, in morning and evening, military, academic, and medieval attire. The Prince had to breakfast, lunch, dine, and sup, with more or less publicity, every twenty-four hours. He had to go twice to races, with fifty or a hundred thousand people about him; to review a small army and make a tour in the Wicklow mountains, of course everywhere receiving addresses under canopies and dining in state under galleries full of spectators. He visited and inspected institutions, colleges, universities, academies, libraries, and cattle shows. He had to take a very active part in assemblies of from several hundred to several thousand dancers, and always to select for his partners the most important personages. . . . He had to listen to many speeches sufficiently to know when and what to answer. He had to examine with respectful interest, pictures, books, antiquities, relics, manuscripts, specimens, bones, fossils, prize beasts, and works of Irish art. He had never to be unequal to the occasion, however different from the last, or however like the last, and whatever his disadvantage as to the novelty or dulness of the matter and the scene."

Some amusing incidents happened. A loyal Irish girl, determined to have a good look at her future King and Queen, defied all rails and barriers, and, mounted on horseback, dashed through the crowd of sightseers and galloped past the Prince and Princess, exclaiming, "Oh, thank you all, I have seen them and shall go home happy now." The Prince, with a smile, raised his hat, which was certainly the most sensible thing he could have done in the circumstances.

THE PRINCE AT THE AGE OF TWENTY-THREE
From a Painting by Weigall, published by Henry Graves and Co.

His Royal Highness has always shown great interest in Ireland and Irish matters, so much so that it has been more than once whispered that he is a Home Ruler. He gave his warm support and help to a fund for the relief of distress in Ireland, and more recently, during the annual show of the Royal Agricultural Society, he took the opportunity to receive and entertain at Sandringham no fewer than three hundred and fifty Irish tenant-farmers.

On their way back from Dublin the Prince and Princess visited North Wales, and on landing at Holyhead they passed along the pier through a double line of aged Welshwomen, who were all wearing the tall hat and national dress of the Principality. At Carnarvon the Prince inaugurated some new waterworks, and after this ceremony the Royal party proceeded to the famous castle, where they were presented with an address from the Council of the National Eisteddfod. The Prince replied in a neat little speech, in which he observed that he and the Princess received the address with peculiar satisfaction on the anniversary of the birth, on 25th April 1284, and in the very birthplace, of the first Prince of Wales, "Edward of Carnarvon," the son of Edward I.

Their Royal Highnesses' fourth child, the Princess Victoria, was born on 6th July, and after a quiet summer spent at Sandringham the Prince and Princess of Wales, attended by a small suite, left Marlborough House in November for a long Continental tour, which extended over some months and enabled them to renew old ties and make new friendships. They spent a few days in Paris, and paid a visit to the Emperor and Empress of the French at Compiègne, where, during a stag hunt organised in honour of His Royal Highness, an accident happened which might easily have cost the Prince of Wales his life. As he was galloping along one of the grassy drives of the forest, a stag rushed from one of the cross-paths and knocked him and his horse completely over. Fortunately he was not hurt, though much bruised and shaken. Without alarming those about him, he again mounted and went on hunting to the end of the day. At this house-party the Prince and Princess had as fellow-guests Marshal Bazaine, Count von Moltke, and a number of other notable people destined to make history.

The Princess's birthday, 1st December, was spent in Denmark. After a short stay there their Royal Highnesses went to Berlin, where a large family party was assembled to meet them, and on 18th January, which is, curiously enough, one of the only two days of the year in which it can be held, a Chapter of the Order of the Black Eagle was convened, and the Prince of Wales was formally invested

CONTINENTAL AND EASTERN TOUR 75

with the Collar of this the highest order in Germany by the King, to whom he was introduced by his brother-in-law, the Crown Prince, and by Prince Albert of Prussia.

Then followed an interesting sojourn in Vienna. The Royal party were splendidly entertained by the Emperor and Empress, a suite of apartments in the Burg having been specially prepared for them.

Five days later the Prince and Princess proceeded to Trieste, where they were joined by Prince Louis of Battenberg, the Duke of Sutherland, Dr. (now Sir) W. H. Russell, and other friends, together with their suite. Their Royal Highnesses embarked on board H.M.S. *Ariadne*, and reached Alexandria on 3rd February 1869. They were met by the usual loyal greetings, addresses, and bouquets presented by the British residents.

Their Royal Highnesses went on to Cairo, where they were received by the Viceroy

THE QUEEN, THE PRINCESS OF WALES,
AND PRINCESS HELENA

Photograph by Hughes and Mullins, Ryde

of Egypt and his Ministers, and before starting on their journey up the Nile the Prince and Princess took the opportunity of witnessing the curious and interesting Procession of the Holy Carpet starting from Cairo on its way to Mecca, which, strangely enough, few of the Europeans who at that time visited Cairo cared to see. Every year there are sent two carpets, one of which goes to Medina to serve as a covering for the tomb of the Prophet, and the other to Mecca to be a covering for Kaabah or the central point of the Mahomedan religion. The Prince and Princess also witnessed the departure of the pilgrims for Mecca, or rather of that portion of the pilgrimage consisting of sheikhs and holy men, escorted by irregular cavalry and artillery, which left the city to join the other pilgrims encamped on the plain outside.

From Cairo the Prince and Princess began their eventful voyage up the Nile. The Viceroy had taken the greatest pains to provide dahabeahs worthy of those whom he desired to honour. The chief barge was occupied by the Prince and Princess and Mrs. Grey, who was in attendance on Her Royal Highness. It was named the *Alexandra*, in compliment to the Princess, and was towed by a steamer flying the Royal Standard and the Ottoman flag side by side, and there was also a kitchen dahabeah attached to it. The suite lived on board another steamer, on which the Royal party daily assembled for breakfast and dinner. On another vessel were the quarters of Murad Pasha and several members of the Duke of Sutherland's party. The store-boat had been very amply equipped with provisions. There were 3000 bottles of champagne, 20,000 bottles of soda-water, 4000 bottles of claret, and plenty of ale, liqueurs, and light wines.

His Royal Highness looked forward to having plenty of sport during the voyage. Accordingly he had taken a large variety of guns of almost every calibre in use, as well as a wherry to be used for approaching land game. For the purpose of capturing crocodiles nets were brought which had been specially made under the superintendence of Sir Samuel Baker. The Prince had also specially arranged for the inclusion in his party of a clever naturalist and taxidermist.

Both the Prince and Princess greatly enjoyed this novel form of yachting, although, unfortunately, bad weather soon set in, and the Royal barge was frequently enveloped in clouds of dust and sand. Notwithstanding this, however, the Prince had plenty of good sport and bagged some very large birds, though the crocodiles were, on the whole, conspicuous by their absence. Soon the Prince's taxidermist could show some very fine specimens of spoonbills, flamingoes, herons, cranes, cormorants, and doves.

During their slow progress up the river the Royal party took frequent excursions, including one to Karnak. On this occasion the Princess rode a milk-white ass, caparisoned in crimson velvet and gold; while the Prince was mounted on a gray mule. It was noticed that the Princess entered with the greatest zest into the exploration and sight-seeing, and there is no doubt that this voyage aided greatly her restoration to health.

Her Royal Highness, however, had one very serious adventure. One night the Prince of Wales, who was on board the steamer, observed a light reflected on the side of the *Alexandra*. He at once gave an alarm, the Princess and Mrs. Grey, who were in the dahabeah, were hurried off to the shore, and the fire, which had been caused by a lighted candle in Prince Louis of Battenberg's cabin, was put out by the Prince and his suite. Had not the quick eye of His Royal Highness discovered the danger a terrible tragedy might have taken place, for the boats were wooden and scorched by an Egyptian sun, while there were, of course, a considerable number of cartridges on board.

The Arabs showed the friendliest feeling to the Prince and Princess. A little Nubian monkey was presented to Her Royal Highness, and the fortunate donor received in exchange an English double-barrelled fowling-piece and some "backsheesh."

Unfortunately the Royal party were to a certain extent worried by inquisitive tourists, who were naturally very anxious to catch a glimpse of them. As usual, the Prince made a point of visiting all specially British institutions, including a mission school.

On their return to Cairo the Prince and Princess attended some native races given by the Viceroy in their honour, and also a theatrical performance.

Then came one of the most interesting episodes of their Royal Highnesses' tour, namely, their visit to the Suez Canal, where they were received and escorted by M. de Lesseps. The works of the Canal Company were by no means completed, but they were being actively carried forward; a large dock, 450 feet long, having been already finished. At Tussum the Prince performed the important ceremony of opening the sluices of the dam across the finished portion of the canal, thus letting the waters of the Mediterranean into the empty basin of the Bitter Lakes. After having seen this interesting sight, the Royal party proceeded by the canal *via* Lake Timsah to Ismailia, even then a great and Frenchified city.

At the end of March the Prince and Princess, accompanied by

their suite, returned to Alexandria and once more embarked on the *Ariadne*, after bidding a very cordial farewell to their Egyptian entertainers.

The *Ariadne* first sighted the minarets and mosques of Constantinople on the morning of 1st April. The Prince and his suite came up on deck attired in full uniform, and the Royal party, including the Princess, made their actual arrival at Constantinople in a new yacht of the Sultan's called the *Pertif Piali*. Their Royal Highnesses were met on the steps of the Palace by the Sultan, the Grand Vizier acting as interpreter, while the Commander of the Faithful led his British guests up the grand staircase and himself showed them the rooms prepared for them in the Salih Bazaar Palace on the north side of the Bosphorus. Every European luxury had been provided. The lattice work, which is always put up across the windows in Turkish houses in order to screen the fair inmates from the rude gaze of outsiders, had been removed and replaced with magnificent silk hangings. All the servants appointed to wait on the Prince and Princess of Wales were Greek and European, except the coachmen, who were French.

Then followed days which must have recalled to the Royal visitors some of the stories in the *Arabian Nights*. The meals at the Salih Bazaar Palace were all served on gold and silver plate studded with gems; a band of eighty-four musicians played during dinner; every morning arrived gorgeous presents from the Sultan, including exquisite flowers and trays laden with fruits and sweets; while, at a clap of the hand, black-coated chibouquejees brought in pipes with amber mouth-pieces of fabulous value, encrusted in diamonds and rubies. There was a complete Turkish bath establishment in the Palace; and the slightest wish expressed by the Prince of Wales was considered an order.

The Prince and Princess witnessed the passing in State of the Sultan, as Commander of the Faithful, to the Mosque Bashiktash amid an unusual display of pomp and ceremony; and while the pageant was passing, little Prince Izzedin, the Heir-Apparent, visited their Royal Highnesses.

The great event of their visit was a State dinner given by the Sultan to the Prince and Princess at the Dolma Baghtche Palace.

CONTINENTAL AND EASTERN TOUR 79

This was the first banquet ever given by a Sultan of Turkey to Christians. It was also remarkable as being the first occasion on which any Minister except a Grand Vizier had ever sat down in a Sultan's presence. The whole Diplomatic Corps were also invited. The table was laid for twenty-four, and the *menu* was composed of Turkish and French dishes.

On the Sunday of their stay at Constantinople the Royal party attended divine service at the Church of the British Embassy, and shortly after were rowed across the Bosphorus to visit the cemetery at Scutari. On the following day the Prince and Princess spent a most amusing couple of hours visiting the native quarter of Stambul *incognito* as "Mr. and Mrs. Williams." They walked through the bazaar and made some purchases, and their identity was never suspected for one moment.

As a very exceptional favour, the Sultan conducted the Princess and Mrs. Grey to his harem. They stayed there an hour and a half, and Her Royal Highness had several interesting conversations with some of the inmates.

On 10th April, after having bidden adieu to the Sultan, their Royal Highnesses started for the Crimea, making their first stay at Sebastopol, where they were courteously received by the Russian authorities, headed by General De Kotzbue, who had been Chief of the Staff to the Commander of Sebastopol, and no one could have shown their Royal Highnesses the sights of the place more competently and with more tact and good feeling.

During the four days that the Prince and Princess stayed in a spot so intensely full of associations to them both, they saw the battlefields of the Alma, of Inkerman, and Balaclava, and they visited the various monuments and memorial chapels. At one village a number of Tartars received the Royal visitors with cheers, and made an offering of bread and salt to the Prince and Princess.

After the four days were over, their Royal Highnesses entertained the Russian General and his staff on board the *Ariadne*, and during dinner the band played "God preserve the Emperor," after which the Royal host proposed the Czar's health, while the General replied with that of the Queen. It is interesting to add that the Russians present treated the Crimean war as a matter of history, quite removed from passion or feeling of any kind. The Prince made a point of visiting the simple house which was at that time still known as Lord Raglan's headquarters, in which is the room where the great commander died. They then joined the *Ariadne* at Yalta, and returned to Constantinople, where they again saw the Sultan for a short time, and entertained the various Ambassadors.

On 20th April the *Ariadne* anchored at Athens, the Prince and Princess receiving a very warm welcome from King George, who hastened on deck to welcome his sister and brother-in-law. A special train was in waiting, and the Royal party soon found themselves in the King's Palace, where they spent a few days in busy sight-seeing, leaving Athens on 23rd April, where the Queen of Greece welcomed her sister-in-law with great warmth. During their stay at Corfu the Prince and Princess enjoyed a much-needed period of repose. The Prince and Princess returned home through Italy, without, however, making any stay in that country. On 12th May they found themselves home again at Marlborough House after an absence of nearly six months.

Among the formal acts of ceremony which the Prince performed during this year (1869) was the unveiling of a statue of the late Mr. George Peabody. In the speech which he delivered on this occasion he alluded in the warmest terms to his feeling of personal friendship towards the United States and his enduring recollection of the reception which had been accorded to him there.

CHAPTER VII

THE PRINCE'S ILLNESS

THE outbreak and progress of the Franco-Prussian war were naturally watched with the keenest interest in Marlborough House. Two of the Prince's own brothers-in-law were serving with the German forces, while, on the other hand, His Royal Highness not only had many close ties with France, but from childhood had always regarded the Emperor and Empress of the French with special affection. When public subscription lists were opened in aid of the ambulances, which distributed medical aid impartially to the sick and wounded on both sides, the Prince gave a liberal donation; and when the Empress Eugénie fled to England, one of the first visits which she received at Chislehurst was from the Prince and Princess of Wales.

As may be easily imagined, the Prince is very popular all over France, and he has had many curious and interesting adventures when going out in the semi-*incognito* which he affects when travelling for pleasure. On one occasion, shortly after the end of the war, His Royal Highness, accompanied by General Teesdale, visited the battlefield of Sedan. He was naturally anxious that his identity should not become known, for French susceptibilities were very keen at that time, and he had no desire to appear to glory over his brother-in-law's brilliant victories. When the time came to pay the hotel bill General Teesdale found with great dismay that he had no ready cash; the Prince was in an equally penniless condition; while any telegram sent would have disclosed the identity of the Royal visitor. At length, after much discussion, the equerry made his way to the local *Mont de Piété* and placed both his own and the Prince's repeater in pawn.

Exactly ten years after the first dread news of the Prince Consort's fatal illness had gone forth, it became known that the Prince of Wales was lying seriously ill at Sandringham. Not very long before, Princess Alice, who was then staying at Sandringham, wrote the following note to the Queen :—

"It is the first time since eleven years that I have spent Bertie's birthday with him, and though we have only three of our own family together, still that is better than nothing, and makes it seem more like a birthday. Bertie and Alix are so kind, and give us so warm a welcome, showing how they like having us, that it feels quite home. Indeed, I pray earnestly that God's blessing may rest on him, and that he may be guided to do what is wise and right, so that he may tide safely through the anxious times that are before him, and in which we now live."

Princess Alice little knew the days and nights of anxious misery that were coming so swiftly upon her brother's peaceful household, and indeed upon the whole nation. The Prince of Wales sickened in London, but as soon as he felt himself to be seriously attacked he insisted on going home to Norfolk, where the disease was pronounced to be typhoid fever.

The Prince, his groom Blegge, and Lord Chesterfield, who had all been at Scarborough with Lord Londesborough, were stricken simultaneously, and public attention was soon wholly concentrated on the three cases. Curiously enough, the groom and the peer both died, though in neither case were any pains or expense spared. Doubtless the Prince's youth and excellent constitution stood him in good stead, but for many days the issue was considered exceedingly doubtful.

His Royal Highness was nursed entirely by the Princess of Wales and Princess Alice, his medical attendants being Doctors Jenner, Gull, Clayton, and Lowe. On the last day of November came a semi-official notification :—

"The Princess of Wales has borne her great trial in the most admirable manner and with singular equanimity. While fully aware of the gravity of the Prince's serious illness, Her Royal Highness has throughout been calm and collected."

But it was well known that the Prince's state was very critical, and soon it was announced that the Queen was going to Sandringham, which she did on 29th November.

Again and again there was a report of a relapse, and the feeling aroused through the United Kingdom was far greater than any public expression of emotion since the death of Princess Charlotte in 1817. In every town, according to the *Times'* reports, crowds waited anxiously for the issue of newspapers containing the latest news of the Prince's condition, and the Government found it expedient to forward the medical bulletins to every telegraph office in the United Kingdom. In the churches of every religious communion, prayers were offered, though almost without hope, for the recovery of the Prince.

At length, on 1st December, the Prince recovered consciousness, and his first remark to those about him was, "This is the Princess's birthday." The next coherent utterance came when he heard that the Queen had been at Sandringham. "Has the Queen come from Scotland? Does she know I am ill?" he asked; but this slight rally did not continue, and soon all the Royal family were summoned to Sandringham. On 9th December the fever had spent itself, but the patient's strength was considered to be exhausted. Special prayers were offered up in all churches for the Prince's recovery; and shortly before the service in St. Mary Magdalene's, Sandringham, the Vicar received the following note from the Princess of Wales:—

"My husband being, thank God, somewhat better, I am coming to church. I must leave, I fear, before the service is concluded, that I may watch by his bedside. Can you not say a few words in prayer in the early part of the service, that I may join with you in prayer for my husband before I return to him?" The Vicar, before reading the Collect, in a voice trembling with emotion, which he vainly strove to suppress, said: "The prayers of the congregation are earnestly sought for His Royal Highness the Prince of Wales, who is now most seriously ill."

The day following, an article in the *Times* commenced: "The Prince still lives and we may still therefore hope"; and so the weary days dragged on. On the 16th it was recorded that the patient had enjoyed a quiet and refreshing sleep, and on the 17th, a Sunday, those of the Royal family who were then at Sandringham were present at church, when, by special request, the Prince and Blegge were recommended to the mercy of God in the same prayer. That same day the Princess visited the poor dying groom, and after his death, which occurred within the next few hours, both she and the Queen found time, in the midst of their terrible anxiety, to visit and comfort his relations.

By Christmas Day the danger may be said to have been over, and on 26th December the Queen wrote the following letter to the nation :—

"The Queen is very anxious to express her deep sense of the touching sympathy of the whole nation on the occasion of the alarming illness of her dear son, the Prince of Wales. The universal feeling shown by her people during those painful, terrible days, and the sympathy evinced by them with herself and her beloved daughter, the Princess of Wales, as well as the general joy at the improvement of the Prince of Wales's state, have made a deep and lasting impression on her heart, which can never be effaced. . . ."

The Princess of Wales and Princess Alice now felt that their patient was well enough for them to leave him for an hour or two in order to assist at the distribution of Christmas gifts to the labourers on the estate. In the ceiling of the room now occupied by the Princess of Wales as a bed-chamber, the mark of an orifice may still be seen from which projected a hook supporting a trapeze, by the aid of which the Prince, when on the slow and weary road to convalescence, could change his position and pull himself up into a sitting posture.

Another memento of the Prince's terrible illness is the brass lectern in the parish church. On it runs an inscription :—

To the glory of God.
A thank-offering for His mercy.
14th December 1871.
Alexandra.

"When I was in trouble I called upon the Lord, and He heard me."

The last bulletin was issued on 14th January, and nine days later Sir William Jenner was gazetted a K.C.B. and Dr. W. Gull was

THE PRINCE'S ILLNESS

created a baronet—rewards which gave particular satisfaction to the nation.

It was whispered at the time that the Prince, under Providence, really owed his recovery to one of those sudden inspirations of genius of which the history of medicine is full. His Royal Highness seemed to be actually *in extremis*, when one of his medical attendants sent in haste for two bottles of old champagne brandy and rubbed the patient with it vigorously all over till returning animation rewarded the doctor's efforts.

The Prince's recovery was hailed with feelings of deep thankfulness by the whole nation, and it was universally deemed appropriate that public thanks should be returned to Almighty God for His great mercy. The utmost interest was taken by all classes of society in the preparations for the proposed National Thanksgiving. Mr. William Longman wrote to the *Times* urging that, as in 1664 and 1678, subscriptions should be invited for the completion of the Cathedral Church of St. Paul in London as a perpetual memorial of His Royal Highness's recovery.

During the interval before the day fixed for the National Thanksgiving, the Prince and Princess paid visits to Windsor and Osborne. When they returned to London one of the first visitors they received was Dr. Stanley, who had now become Dean of Westminster. It was resolved that their Royal Highnesses should attend a private service of thanksgiving in the Abbey, which the Dean thus describes in a letter to an intimate correspondent :—

"I went to Marlborough House to suggest, through Fisher and Keppel, that the Prince of Wales should come. He consented at once, and it was agreed that he, the Princess, and the Crown Prince of Denmark, and if in town, Prince Alfred, should come. I kept it a secret except from the Canons. We met them at the great Western door ; the nave (as usual) was quite clear. They walked in with me, and took their places on my right. I preached on Psalm cxxii. 1. The Prince of Wales heard every word, and has decided that it shall be published, which it will be, and you shall have a copy. It was one of those rare occasions on which I was able to say all that I wished to say. They were conducted again to the West door, and departed."

86 THE PRINCE OF WALES

The day fixed for the public National Thanksgiving in St. Paul's was 27th February, and never, save perhaps on 22nd June 1897, did the Queen and the Prince and Princess of Wales receive a more splendid and heartfelt ovation. Thirteen thousand people were

THANKSGIVING DAY, 1872 : THE SCENE AT TEMPLE BAR
From the " Illustrated London News"

admitted to the Cathedral, among them being most of the notabilities of the day, including all the great officers of State.

The procession set out from Buckingham Palace at twelve o'clock. First came the Speaker, the Lord Chancellor, and the Commander-in-Chief, in their carriages, followed by nine Royal equipages, in the last of which sat the Queen, dressed in black velvet trimmed with

THE PRINCE'S ILLNESS

broad bands of white ermine, the Princess of Wales in blue silk covered with black lace, the Prince of Wales in the uniform of a British general and wearing the Collars of the Orders of the Garter and the Bath, Prince Albert Victor, then a boy of eight, and Princess Beatrice.

In the Green Park the procession was greeted by an army of 30,000 children, who sang the National Anthem as the Royal carriages drove by.

St. Paul's was reached at one o'clock, and the Royal party were received at the great West door by the Dean and Chapter. The Queen passed up the nave leaning on the arm of the Prince, who conducted Her Majesty to a pew which had been specially prepared for the occasion.

The service began with the "Te Deum," and after some prayers a special form of thanksgiving which had been officially drawn up was said. Then the Archbishop of Canterbury preached a short sermon from the text, Romans xii. 5, ".Members one of another." The service concluded with a thanksgiving hymn which had been specially written for the occasion. The proceedings were over by two o'clock, and the procession returned by a different route, along Holborn and Oxford Street, in the presence of an enthusiastic crowd said to be the largest ever collected in London. As the poet sings:—

> Bear witness, thou memorable day,
> When, pale as yet, and fever-worn, the Prince,
> Who scarce had plucked his flickering life again
> From halfway down the shadow of the grave,
> Past through the people and their love,
> And London roll'd one tide of joy thro' all
> Her trebled millions and loud leagues of men.

Two days later the Queen wrote from Buckingham Palace to Mr. Gladstone, who was then Prime Minister, one of those touching letters which have on many occasions drawn still more closely together the ties of loyalty and affection between Her Majesty and her people. The Queen wrote that she was anxious "to express publicly her own personal very deep sense of the reception she and her dear children met with on Tuesday, the 27th of February, from millions of her subjects on her way to and from St. Paul's. Words are too weak for the Queen to say how very deeply touched and gratified she has been by the immense enthusiasm and affection exhibited towards her dear son and herself, from the highest down to the lowest, in the long progress through the capital, and she would earnestly wish to convey her warmest and most heartfelt thanks to the whole nation for this great demonstration of loyalty. The Queen, as well as her son and dear daughter-in-law, felt that the whole nation

THANKSGIVING DAY, 1872 : THE PROCESSION UP LUDGATE HILL
From the "Illustrated London News"

joined with them in thanking God for sparing the beloved Prince of Wales's life. . . ."

The impression made by the Prince's illness and marvellous recovery upon the Royal family in general is well illustrated by the following passage from a letter written by Princess Alice to her mother in December 1872 :—

"That our good, sweet Alix should have been spared this terrible grief, when this time last year it seemed so imminent, fills my heart with gratitude for her dear sake, as for yours, his children and ours. . . . The 14th will now be a day of mixed recollections and feelings to us, a day hallowed in our family, when one great spirit ended his work on earth . . . and when another was left to fulfil his duty and mission, God grant, for the welfare of his own family and of thousands."

CHAPTER VIII

1873-1875

THE year 1873 was spent on the whole very quietly by the Prince and Princess of Wales. His Royal Highness took up once more the thread of his public life which had been interrupted for a considerable time by his illness and convalescence. Accompanied by his brother, Prince Arthur, he went to Vienna in May to represent the British Royal family at the opening of the International Exhibition there. In June the Prince and Princess were deeply grieved to hear of the death of the infant son of Princess Alice of Hesse, who was killed by falling out of the window of his mother's room in the Royal Palace at Darmstadt. But their Royal Highnesses, though the blow was exceptionally severe owing to their fond affection for Princess Alice, were compelled in the midst of their grief to devote a considerable portion of their time to entertaining the Shah. A great dinner was given in his honour at Marlborough House, and the Prince of Wales spared neither time nor trouble in doing honour to our distinguished Oriental visitor.

A pleasant glimpse of the home life at Sandringham about this time is given in the following letters from the witty and eloquent Archbishop Magee (then Bishop of Peterborough), written to his wife:—

"SANDRINGHAM, *6th December* 1873.

" . . . I arrived just as they were all at tea in the entrance hall, and had to walk in, all seedy and dishevelled from my day's journey, and sit down beside the Princess of Wales, with Disraeli on the other side of me, and sundry lords and ladies round the

THE QUEEN, WITH THE PRINCES ALBERT VICTOR AND GEORGE, AND THE
PRINCESS VICTORIA OF WALES

From the Painting by James Sant, R.A.

table. The Prince received me very kindly, and certainly has most winning and gracious manners. The Princess seems smaller and thinner than I remember her at Dublin. They seem to be pleasant and domesticated, with little state and very simple ways."

"*7th December* 1873.

"Just returned from church, where I preached for twenty-six minutes (Romans viii. 28). The church is a very small country one close to the grounds. The house, as I saw it by daylight, is a handsome country house of red stone with white facings, standing well and looking quietly comfortable and suitable. I find the company pleasant and civil, but we are a curious mixture. Two Jews, Sir A. Rothschild and his daughter; an ex-Jew, Disraeli; a Roman Catholic, Colonel Higgins; an Italian duchess who is an Englishwoman, and her daughter brought up as a Roman Catholic and now turning Protestant; a set of young lords, and a bishop. The Jewess came to church; so did the half-Protestant young lady. Dizzy did the same, and was profuse in his praises of my sermon. We are all to lunch together in a few minutes, the children dining with us. They seem, the two I saw in church, nice, clever-looking little bodies, and very like their mother."

The Prince and Princess of Wales represented the Queen at the marriage of the Duke of Edinburgh and the Grand Duchess Marie of Russia in January 1874. The English marriage service was performed by Dean Stanley, who wrote to the Queen an interesting letter describing the Imperial wedding, in which he mentioned how much he had been struck, both in the chapel and at the subsequent banquet, by the singular difference in character and expression of the four future kings, the Prince of Wales, the Crown Prince of Prussia, the Cesarewitch, and the Crown Prince of Denmark, who were all present.

On the Sunday following the wedding the Prince and Princess of Wales attended the service at the English Church in St. Petersburg, and the Dean preached on the marriage feast at Cana in Galilee, much the same sermon which he had preached in the Chapel-Royal at Whitehall on the Sunday following the marriage of the Prince and Princess of Wales. During this visit to Russia the

Prince and Princess were received with unusual distinction, and a grand parade of troops was held in His Royal Highness's honour.

The Prince of Wales dined in the Middle Temple Hall on Grand Night of Trinity term in 1874. On this occasion His Royal Highness humorously expressed the opinion that it was a good thing for the profession at large, and for the public in general, that he had never practised at the Bar, for he could never have been an ornament to it, in saying which his modesty probably led him astray, for he is a thoughtful and lucid speaker, and his habits of method and order would certainly have stood him in good stead if he had been compelled to apply his mind to any profession.

When the Prince and Princess were first married they always gave two great balls at Marlborough House each year—one on the anniversary of their wedding day, and one at the close of the London season. But the most splendid entertainment ever given by the Prince and Princess was the great fancy dress ball in July 1874. Over fourteen hundred invitations were sent out, and the Royal host and hostess made no stipulations as to the choice of costume, leaving it to individual taste. The Princess wore a Venetian dress, and was attended by her two young sons as pages. The Prince appeared as Charles I., wearing a costume exactly copied from the famous Vandyke picture, that is, a maroon satin and velvet suit, partly covered with a short black velvet cloak, while the black hat, trimmed with one long white feather, was looped up with an aigrette of brilliants. He also wore high buff boots, long spurs and sword, while round his neck hung the Collar of the Garter.

Many of the costumes worn were very interesting and curious. In the Fairy Tale Quadrille, the Earl of Rosebery, then quite a youth, was Blue Beard; Mr. Albert (now Earl) Grey, Puss in Boots; and the Duke of Connaught, the Beast. Lord Charles and Lord Marcus Beresford were a couple of Court jesters. The only person present who was not in fancy dress was Benjamin Disraeli, then Prime Minister. He wore the official dress of a Privy Councillor.

That same year the Prince and Princess visited Birmingham for the first time, being received by the then mayor, Mr. Joseph

Chamberlain, who was at the time credited with being so advanced a Republican that many fears were expressed that he might behave with scant courtesy to his Royal guests, and bets were even taken as to whether he would consent to shake hands with the Prince of Wales! However, these prognostications proved groundless, and the people of Birmingham gave an unparalleled demonstration of loyalty which gratified their Royal Highnesses extremely.

The festivities of the following Christmas were overshadowed by the death at Sandringham from inflammation of the lungs of Colonel Grey, who had been for some time a valued member of the Prince's household. It was with reference to this sad loss that Princess Alice wrote to the Queen:—"Dear Bertie's true and constant heart suffers on such occasions, for he can be constant in friendship, and all who serve him, serve him with warm attachment."

In 1875 the death of Canon Kingsley came as a great blow to the Prince and Princess of Wales, who were both fondly attached to the famous writer.

The Prince's Indian Tour, 1875

CHAPTER IX

THE PRINCE OF WALES'S TOUR IN INDIA

Lord Canning, the great Viceroy of India, once told the Prince Consort how desirable he thought it that the Prince of Wales should, when grown up, visit Queen Victoria's Eastern Empire, and later on, those who had the privilege of the young Prince's friendship were well aware that an Indian tour had become one of his most ardent wishes.

But the project of the Heir-Apparent's visit to India only really took shape early in 1875, and on 20th March it was publicly announced that the Prince of Wales contemplated this journey, the Marquis of Salisbury at the same time making an official announcement to the Council of India of the intended event. The Council passed a resolution that the expenditure actually incurred in India should be charged on the revenues of that country.

Curiously enough, a great deal of hostile feeling was aroused by the announcement of this Royal tour. On 17th July a great meeting was held in Hyde Park to protest against the grant of money which was then being sanctioned by Parliament to defray the expenses of the journey. Many people went so far as to declare that they would have acquiesced in the passing of the vote had the Heir-Apparent's visit to his mother's Eastern dominions been a "State visit" instead of a mere "pleasure trip." And yet it need hardly be pointed out that, greatly as the Prince looked forward to his tour, the journey was likely to prove anything but a mere "pleasure trip" to India's Royal visitor. He and those about him well knew that from the moment he landed at Bombay till the day he left India he would not only constantly remain *en évidence*, but he also expected to conciliate the many different races with which he was going to be brought in contact when passing through the various Indian States.

There were many points to be considered about the tour. The rules and regulations which had sufficed for the Prince in Canada and the Colonies were inapplicable to India. One notable feature of Oriental manners is the exchange of presents between visitors and hosts, and it was early arranged that His Royal Highness's luggage should contain £40,000 worth of presents to be distributed among the great feudatory and other potentates who would have the honour of entertaining or at any rate of meeting the Prince.

It was also arranged that the Prince was to be guest of the Viceroy, Lord Northbrook, from the moment he landed on Indian soil; and, roughly speaking, it was estimated that the expenses of the Prince's reception alone would probably come to about £30,000. The estimate made by the Admiralty for the expenses of the voyage to and from India and the movements of the fleet in connection with the Royal visit came to £52,000; while for the personal expenses of the Prince's visit a vote of £60,000 was included in the estimate submitted to the House of Commons when in Committee of Supply. However, here again this suggestion did not meet with universal approval when the necessary resolution was brought forward in the House. Mr. Fawcett, afterwards Postmaster-General, raised a discussion, basing his objections to the vote partly on sentimental and partly on economic grounds. However, he only found thirty-three members to agree with him, and the vote was passed. During the debate, Mr. Disraeli, who was then Prime Minister, drew a very remarkable picture of the extraordinary pomp and circumstance with which the Prince was about to be surrounded.

It was felt better that His Royal Highness should go as Heir-Apparent of the Crown, and not as the representative of Her Majesty, but, as might have been expected, these fine distinctions were not understood in India, and the Prince was expected to do just as much as he would have done in a more directly official capacity.

Before starting on his tour the Prince of Wales thoroughly studied the subject of India and her peoples, and he even made himself acquainted with the peculiarities of every one of the large Indian cities where he would be expected to receive and answer addresses.

The question of the suite was, as may be imagined, very important. It was early decided that Sir Bartle Frere, whose name was familiar to millions of the inhabitants of India, should accompany the Prince of Wales, and the Duke of Sutherland was also asked to join the party. Of His Royal Highness's private friends, the Earl of Aylesford, Lord (now Earl) Carrington, Colonel (now General) Owen Williams, and Lieutenant (now Admiral) Lord Charles Beresford, also accepted an invitation to be of the party. Then came the official Household, consisting of Lord Suffield; Colonel Ellis, the Prince's equerry, to whom was confided the delicate question of the giving and receiving of presents; General (now Sir Dighton) Probyn, to whom were left the arrangements for horses, travelling, and shooting parties; and Mr. (now Sir Francis) Knollys, the Prince's private secretary. Canon Duckworth went as chaplain, and Dr. (now Sir Joseph) Fayrer as medical man. Mr. Albert Grey (now Earl Grey) went as private secretary to Sir Bartle Frere, Mr. S. P. Hall accompanied the Prince in order to sketch the incidents of the tour, while Lord Alfred Paget was specially commissioned by Her Majesty to join the suite. Dr. W. H. (now Sir William) Russell, the famous war correspondent, who was temporarily attached to the suite as honorary private secretary to the Prince, wrote on his return a very interesting account of the tour, entitled "The Prince of Wales's Tour in India," which has remained the standard authority on the subject.

On the day that His Royal Highness left Sandringham, amid many demonstrations of good-will and wishings of God-speed from his country neighbours, he presented the Princess with a team of Corsican ponies and a miniature drag. The Prince spent the last

H

few days of his stay in England with the Princess and his children at Marlborough House. On the Sunday before his departure they were all present at divine service in Westminster Abbey, and the next day His Royal Highness went to say good-bye to his old friend Dean Stanley, who, in a letter to an intimate correspondent, gave the following vivid description of the visit :—

"On the Sunday night we had a message to say that the Prince and Princess of Wales would come to take leave of us at 3.30 P.M. the next day. They came about 4 P.M., having been detained by the members of the family coming to Marlborough House.

"They brought all the five children, wishing, the Prince said, to have them all with him as long as possible.

"They all came up, and remained about twenty minutes. Fanny was in the back library, and the children, after being for a few minutes with Augusta, who was delighted to see them, went to her.

"The Prince and Princess remained with Augusta and me. A. talked with all her usual animation. They were both extremely kind. The Princess looked inexpressibly sad. There was nothing much said of interest, chiefly talking of the voyage, etc. As I took him downstairs, he spoke of the dangers—but calmly and rationally, saying that, of course, the precautions must be left to those about him. I said to him, 'I gave you my parting benediction in the Abbey yesterday.' 'Yes,' he replied, 'I saw it. Thank you.'

"Later on in the evening Augusta wished me to telegraph our renewed thanks and renewed good wishes to the *Castalia* at Dover. I did so, and at 11 P.M. there came back a telegram from him : 'Many thanks for your kind message. God bless both of you ! Just off for Calais ! ' "

The Prince of Wales started from London on 11th October, immense popular interest being taken in the event. Huge crowds assembled long before the departure of the special train from Charing Cross, and the Prince and Princess were wildly cheered. The Princess accompanied her husband as far as Calais, and then the Prince travelled across the Continent *incognito*, meeting his suite, who had started a few days previously, at Brindisi.

The eventful journey was made in the *Serapis*, one of the old

TOUR IN INDIA 99

large Indian troopships, and the voyage was very successful from every point of view. The Royal party spent a few days at Athens, where the Prince was entertained by his brother-in-law, the King of Greece, to whom he had brought a number of gifts from Sandringham, including an Alderney bull and cow, a ram and sheep, several British pigs, and a number of horses.

From the Piræus the *Serapis* proceeded to Egypt, and His Royal Highness invested Prince Tewfik, the Khedive's eldest son,

EMBARKATION ON BOARD THE "SERAPIS" AT BRINDISI

with the Order of the Star of India. From there the Prince went on without interruption.

As the *Serapis* steamed onwards the various programmes of the Prince of Wales's progress through India were submitted to His Royal Highness, and even the addresses which were to be presented to him were shown and his answers were carefully prepared; in fact, before he left Aden, His Royal Highness knew with what words the Corporation of Bombay would receive him.

As may be easily imagined, all India was by now in a ferment of excitement, and the official world were very much concerned at the immense responsibility placed upon them by the mother-country. Four officers, of whom two had obtained the Victoria Cross, were carefully selected and commissioned to look after the comfort and the safety of the Prince and of his suite, Major Bradford being entrusted with the responsible task of attending to the safety of the Royal visitor's own person.

The question as to how the Prince was to make his first appearance in Bombay was keenly discussed, and at one time it was thought that splendidly caparisoned elephants would form the most fitting mode of transport from the landing-stage to Government House, but finally the party went in carriages. Among the cargo of the *Serapis* were three valuable horses, specially chosen from the Marlborough House stables, which had been regularly taken to the Zoo, in order to be accustomed to the sight of the wild beasts and reptiles which they were likely to meet with in India.

At last it was noised abroad that the *Serapis* had been sighted, and the Viceroy, Lord Northbrook (now the Earl of Northbrook), went out to meet His Royal Highness, returning to Bombay in order to receive the Prince on landing. There was a good deal of discreet curiosity as to which of them would give precedence to the other, for of course the Viceroy represents Her Majesty, and so was entitled to take precedence, but Lord Northbrook, with considerable tact, unobtrusively gave his Royal guest the first place.

The moment the Prince of Wales emerged from the dockyard a salute was fired, and at every station in India, whether important or obscure, the signal was given by telegraph for a Royal salute wherever there were guns to fire it.

While actually in Bombay His Royal Highness and his suite became the guests of the Governor, Sir Philip Woodhouse, and it was there that two days after his arrival in India the Prince celebrated his thirty-fourth birthday, the first object which met his eyes in the morning being a charming portrait of the Princess, which had been specially entrusted to Sir Bartle Frere by Her Royal Highness. On this eventful day the glories and the fatigues of the Prince's Indian tour may be said to have begun.

The Royal birthday was duly honoured all over Hindustan at noon, and although the heat, even at 8 A.M., had been very considerable, the Prince was compelled to hold a great reception in full dress, that is to say, in a uniform of English cloth loaded with lace and buttoned up to the throat. The scene was very impressive. The Prince during the reception was seated on a silver throne, and everything was done to invest the affair with the greatest pomp and circumstance. His suite all stood round him in full uniform; behind the throne was a portrait of the Queen; and although the Prince was not supposed to hold durbars, the ceremony being simply styled a private visit or reception, it was in every way as impressive and remarkable as if it had carried full official significance.

An immense number of native Princes and Rajahs paid their respects in person to their future Sovereign. The first potentate presented to His Royal Highness was the Rajah of Kholapur, a child of twelve years old, the ruler of nearly a million people. The little Rajah was attired in purple velvet and white muslin encrusted with gems, his turban containing a King's ransom of pearls and rubies. In spite of his extreme youth the Indian Prince remained perfectly serious, and went through the somewhat complicated ceremonies with perfect self-possession.

After the last Rajah had departed, the Prince had a long talk with the Viceroy, and then made his way to the *Serapis*, where he had the pleasure of seeing the crew enjoying the birthday dinner provided by himself. He also cut a birthday cake, and looked over the telegrams just received from Sandringham. That same evening was held a great reception, to which naturally the British officials and residents came in great force.

The next few days were also equally well filled. The Prince had to pay elaborate return visits to the chiefs and Rajahs who had attended his reception, and it was then that His Royal Highness was enabled to show his tact and the extraordinary knowledge he had acquired of their complicated ranks and genealogies; indeed, he greatly pleased several important Rajahs by showing that he had heard of the antiquity of their families, and by graciously alluding to the gallant deeds of their ancestors. The British people of Bombay had organised a great dinner for the sailors of the fleet, and, much to their gratification, the Prince consented to attend the banquet. Not content with a mere formal glance at the proceedings,

His Royal Highness mounted a plank, and with a glass in his hand, exclaimed to the delighted men, of whom there were over two thousand present, "My lads, I am glad to meet you all. I drink your good health, and a happy voyage home."

The Prince of Wales took the opportunity of laying the foundation-stone of the Elphinstone Docks, the ceremony being carried out with Masonic honours, and it was considered very interesting and significant that among members of the craft present were Parsees, Mahomedans, and Hindus.

During the month of November the Prince visited Poona, where he held a review, and visited the Court of the Gaikwar of Baroda. There a fine elephant was prepared for his use. The animal was of extraordinary size, and the howdah on which the Prince rode was said to have cost four lakhs of rupees. His Royal Highness held a reception at the Residency, and had his first sight of Indian sport, for he attended a cheetah hunt, himself killing a fine buck, and much enjoying his day's sport. About the same time he also joined a pig-sticking expedition, a very popular Indian sport, and at last, to his great satisfaction, had the opportunity of "getting his spear," in other words, of killing a wild boar.

Then, returning to Bombay, the Royal party once more took up their quarters on the *Serapis*, where the Prince spent the Princess's birthday. From Bombay he found time to visit the Portuguese settlement of Goa, and thence went on to Ceylon, where he inspected a tea plantation, and where the peepul planted by him in commemoration of his visit is still proudly shown to the ubiquitous globe-trotter.

At Madras the Prince of Wales had a splendid reception, spending, however, 14th December, the anniversary of his father's death, in retirement at Guindy Park, the country seat of the Governor, eight miles from the city.

Christmas Day was spent in Calcutta, where an immense programme was gone through, including a considerable number of public ceremonies, the holding of audiences, and last, but not least, a *levée*, at which both natives and Europeans were present. After the Prince and the Viceroy had attended divine service in the Cathedral, His Royal Highness entertained a large party at lunch in the *Serapis*. His health was drunk with Highland honours, and many messages were exchanged between himself and "home." On the afternoon of the same day the Royal party drove out to the Viceregal Lodge at Barrackpur.

The most important ceremony attended by His Royal Highness in India, namely, a Chapter of the Order of the Star of India, at which the Prince acted as High Commissioner, was held on New Year's Day, 1876. His Royal Highness wore a field-marshal's uniform, almost concealed beneath the folds of his sky-blue satin mantle, the train of which was carried by two naval cadets, who wore cocked hats over their powdered wigs, blue satin cloaks, trunk hose, and shoes with rosettes. The Chapter tent was carpeted with cloth of gold with the Royal Arms emblazoned in the centre. An immense number of the Companions of the Order attended, forming a most impressive procession, walking two and two, one half native and the other European. The Begum of Bhopal, the first Knight Grand Commander, had a procession all to herself. She was veiled and swathed in brocades and silks, over which was folded the light blue satin robe of the Order.

The Prince took his seat on the daïs, and after the roll of the Order had been read, each member standing up as his name was called, the Chapter was declared open, and His Royal Highness directed the investiture to proceed. Never had such a gathering been seen in India. Among those present were Lord Napier of Magdala, "Political" Maitland, the Maharajah of Kashmir, and the Rajah of Patiala, who wore the great Sancy diamond in his turban.

As each investiture took place, seventeen guns were fired, and the secretary proclaimed aloud the titles of the newly-made Knight Grand Commander or Companion as the case might be. The pageant was incomparably splendid, the close of the ceremony being quite as fine as the beginning, for the Knights Grand Cross, the Knights Grand Commanders, and the Companions all formed once more in a procession in the reverse order of their entry.

At the close of the Prince's visit to Calcutta His Royal Highness began his journeys by rail. At Benares he visited the famous Temples, and the Golden Pool, going from thence by steamer to the old port of Rammagar, where he and his suite were splendidly received by the Maharajah, who presented him with some very costly shawls and brocades, together with what is to an Indian the very highest proof of regard, namely his own walking-stick, a thick staff mounted with gold.

At Lucknow the Prince laid the foundation-stone of a memorial to the natives who fell in the defence of the Residency. On this occasion His Royal Highness took the opportunity of paying a well-deserved tribute to the faithful soldiers of the native army. Some of the veterans were presented to him, and they were not allowed to be hurried by, ragged, squalid, or unclean; indeed, the Prince insisted on exchanging a few words with several of them.

While at Lucknow His Royal Highness took part in a pig-sticking expedition, at which Lord Carrington's left collar-bone was broken, and curiously enough, Lord Napier of Magdala met with a precisely similar accident on the same day.

From Delhi the Prince proceeded to Cawnpore, a spot he had been extremely anxious to visit, in common with many less illustrious tourists. His Royal Highness, after a drive to the site of the old cantonments, where the heroic defence took place, made his way to the Memorial Church, where he stopped close to the gateway which no native may pass through. There the Prince alighted, and, with signs of deep emotion, walked to the spot which marks the place of the fatal well. There was deep silence as he read aloud in a low voice the touching words, "To the memory of a great company of Christian people, principally women and children, who were cruelly slaughtered here."

On returning to Delhi the Prince held a *levée*, attended by hundreds of British officers, at the close of which several notabilities of the native army were presented. The next day a great review was held, Lord Napier of Magdala entertaining the Prince at his own camp. Delhi was illuminated, and no trouble was spared in showing what was once the capital city of India to Her Majesty's Heir-Apparent.

Some interesting hours were spent at Agra, where His Royal Highness went to see the Taj illuminated, the beautiful marble "Queen of Sorrow" erected by the Shah Jehan in memory of his

much-loved wife, Moomtaz i Mahul, who died in childbirth of
her eighth child. The Prince was so greatly charmed with the

THE PRINCE'S VISIT TO THE CAWNPORE MEMORIAL

beauty of the Taj, lit up by myriad lights, that he would not return
to the city till nearly midnight. All through the journeys and
expeditions which immediately followed, His Royal Highness could

not forget what he had seen, and before finally leaving the district he paid one more visit to the famous tomb, seeing it this time not illuminated, but by the beautiful full Indian moonlight.

The Prince shot his first tiger on 5th February in the neighbourhood of Jeypur. Then he returned through Lucknow, Cawnpore, and Allahabad. At Jubbulpur His Royal Highness went through the prison, and had some talk with seven Thugs who had been thirty-five years in confinement, and whose life in the first instance had only been spared because they had turned Queen's evidence. The Prince questioned them as to their hideous trade, and one man, a villainous-looking individual, answered proudly, in reply to the question as to how many people he had murdered, "Sixty-seven."

The Prince of Wales and his suite left Bombay for home on 13th March, just seventeen weeks after the *Serapis* had first dropped anchor in Bombay harbour. During those four months His Royal Highness had travelled close on 8000 miles by land and 2500 miles by sea, and during that time the Prince had become acquainted with more Rajahs than had all the Viceroys who had ever reigned over India, and he had seen more of the country than had any living Englishman.

The intelligence that the Queen was about to assume the title of Empress of India had become known before the *Serapis* left Bombay, and caused the Prince great gratification. Curiously enough, His Royal Highness met Lord Lytton, who was on his way out to Hindustan to succeed Lord Northbrook as Viceroy, when the *Serapis* was going through the Suez Canal.

The Royal party spent five days in Egypt. By 6th April Malta was in sight, and the Prince was received there with great enthusiasm, as was also the case at Gibraltar, where His Royal Highness had the pleasure of meeting the Duke of Connaught. From there the *Serapis* proceeded by easy stages round Spain, the Prince taking the opportunity of visiting Seville, Cordova, Madrid, the Escurial, Lisbon, and Cintra. At Madrid King Alphonso came to meet the Prince at the station, and they drove together to the Palace, going from there to Toledo in order that His Royal Highness might visit the famous manufactory of Toledo blades.

As the *Serapis* anchored near Yarmouth the Prince of Wales was informed that the Princess and the Royal children had come to meet him on board the *Enchantress*. His Royal Highness immediately went on board their ship, bringing the Princess and their children back with him a quarter of an hour later on to the *Serapis*, the Royal party landing an hour afterwards at Plymouth.

It need hardly be pointed out that the Prince of Wales received a very remarkable number of gifts during his tour in India. The cost of a gift made to the Prince of Wales by a native Prince was supposed to be strictly limited to £2000 in value, but in many cases this restriction was evaded by the present being priced at a nominal sum, the real value being anything from £5000 to £30,000. As an actual fact the splendid collection brought home by the Prince, which is his own personal property, is said to be worth half a million sterling.

Some time after his return home His Royal Highness kindly allowed his Indian gifts to be exhibited to the public. They are now scattered over Marlborough House and Sandringham, a considerable portion of them finding a permanent resting-place in the Indian room of Marlborough House. There also are carefully stored away in solid silver cylinders all the addresses received by the Prince during his eventful Indian tour.

The Prince, who takes the very keenest interest in live animals, brought back quite a menagerie with him from India, and the portion of the *Serapis* assigned to His Royal Highness's pets was for the time being a veritable Zoo, for there were tigers, elephants, ostriches, leopards, birds, ponies, cattle, monkeys, dogs and horses, some of which are still spending a peaceful old age at Sandringham.

There can be no doubt that from a political point of view the Prince's tour was a great success, doing much indirectly to consolidate the British power in India. It is also a curious commentary on the objections raised by the economy party to the visit that no less a sum than £250,000 was spent in London alone by native Princes in buying presents for His Royal Highness.

The principal incident of the voyage home had been a farewell dinner given by the officers of the *Serapis* to the Prince of Wales and his suite when the vessel was nearing harbour.

The table was laid for forty on the main deck (called the Windsor Long Walk), which was decorated with flags, trophies of arms, and ornaments. After the Queen had been honoured, Captain Glyn proposed the Prince's health and begged him to accept an album as a keepsake from himself and his officers. It contained, besides a large photograph of every officer, photographed groups of the men and the Guard of Honour, views of different parts of the ship, and photographs of a few favourite animals.

The real popularity of the Prince's visit to India was significantly proved by the popular demonstrations which awaited him on his return. Enthusiastic greetings of welcome hailed him in the evening both at Victoria Station and in his drive round by Grosvenor Place, Piccadilly, and St. James's Street to meet the Queen at Buckingham Palace. The appearance of the Prince and Princess at the Royal Italian Opera in the evening, within two hours of their reaching home, was a particularly graceful act of consideration. Nothing could surpass the enthusiasm with which their Royal Highnesses were greeted when they were seen in the Royal box.

During the days that followed, their Royal Highnesses received congratulatory visits from all the members of the Royal Family then in England, and from many distinguished personages. On the Sunday after the Prince's return, His Royal Highness, accompanied by the Princess, the Duke of Edinburgh, and the Duke of Connaught, attended divine service at Westminster Abbey in the afternoon, when special thanksgivings were offered up for the safe return of the Prince from India.

Soon afterwards His Royal Highness was entertained at a banquet and ball given by the Corporation of the City of London at the Guildhall. The temporary building erected for this brilliant assembly, to which over five thousand were invited, occupied the whole of Guildhall Yard. The reception hall was on the basement floor, the ballroom being built above it, and was beautifully decorated and draped with Oriental hangings. A daïs had been erected for their Royal Highnesses; and the scene is described as a combination of quaintly mediæval magnificence with modern luxury and elegance. The reception ceremony took place in the new library of the Guild-

TOUR IN INDIA 109

hall, where an address of welcome in a golden casket of Indian design was presented to His Royal Highness by the Lord Mayor. The Prince, in a brief reply, said that it was his highest reward and his greatest pride to have received from the citizens of London and

THE PRINCE IN 1876
From a Drawing by Sargent

his countrymen such a welcome at the termination of a visit which had been undertaken with the view to strengthening the ties that bound India to our common country. The invitation tickets for this brilliant function were both beautiful and appropriate, the Star of India and the Taj Mahal at Agra figuring prominently in the design.

Among the other entertainments given in honour of the Prince's return may be mentioned a concert at the Albert Hall. The Prince and Princess on their arrival were received by a Guard of Honour of 120 bluejackets from the *Serapis*, the *Raleigh*, and the *Osborne*, under the command of Captain Carr Glyn, and in the vestibule were all the Council of the Albert Hall, wearing the Windsor uniform. At their head was the Duke of Edinburgh in naval uniform. The vast hall was crowded with a distinguished audience.

CHAPTER X

QUIET YEARS OF PUBLIC WORK, 1876-87—VISIT TO IRELAND—
THE QUEEN'S JUBILEE

THE year 1876 was marked, in addition to the Prince of Wales's return from India, by a curious example of His Royal Highness's tact and courage. The Prince consented to preside at the special Jubilee Festival of the Licensed Victuallers' Asylum, and this action aroused an extraordinary amount of feeling in temperance circles. Before the day of the festival the Prince of Wales received more than 200 petitions from all over the kingdom begging him to withdraw his consent. His Royal Highness, however, attended the festival, and in his speech pointedly referred to his critics, urging that he was there, not to encourage the consumption of alcoholic liquors, but to support an excellent charity, which had enjoyed the patronage of his honoured father.

It is interesting to note the manner in which the Prince of Wales always refers to his father, with whom he undoubtedly has far more in common than is generally supposed. Perhaps the most conspicuous taste shared by the father and the son is a really keen and personal interest in exhibitions of all kinds. This was probably first realised by those about him twenty years ago, when His Royal Highness accepted the onerous duties of Executive President of the British Commission of the Paris Exhibition of 1878. He threw himself with ardour into this work almost immediately after his return from India, and during a short visit which he paid to France in that spring he received a considerable number of official personages connected with the approaching exhibition.

The Prince, accompanied by the Princess, unveiled in the following

July a statue of Alfred the Great at Wantage, the birthplace of the famous King. The statue was the gift of Colonel Loyd-Lindsay (now Lord Wantage), the sculptor being Count Gleichen (Prince Victor of Hohenlohe-Langenburg). The Prince of Wales is a lineal descendant of King Alfred by the intermarriage of the Saxon with the Norman reigning houses in the eleventh century, and it was most appropriate that he should have been invited to perform the ceremony.

In January 1878 the Prince of Wales, accompanied by Prince Louis Napoleon, visited the Duke of Hamilton at Hamilton Palace, in Lanarkshire. The Crown Prince of Austria was also a guest of His Grace at the time. The Prince greatly enjoyed this visit to the premier Peer of Scotland, who is of the ancient lineage of Scottish Royalty. The Royal visitors enjoyed some excellent sport in the historic Cadzow Forest—*Cadyow* having been granted by King Robert the Bruce after the battle of Bannockburn to Sir Gilbert Hamilton, the ancestor of the present Duke. Here still remain the few old oaks of the once great Caledonian Forest, immortalised by Sir Walter Scott in his ballad of "Cadyow Castle"; and here are also the wild white bulls of the same breed as preserved at Chillingham, and the famous Cadzow herd of wild cattle. The Royal visitors were deeply interested in all that was to be seen here, and greatly enjoyed their visit.

This year of 1878, so brilliant in Paris, brought to the British Royal family a bereavement which can only be compared for its suddenness and bitterness with the death of the Prince Consort. The Grand Duchess of Hesse (Princess Alice), after nursing her children through a malignant diphtheria, herself fell a victim to the same dread disease on the very anniversary of her father's death. The blow fell with peculiar severity on the Prince and Princess of Wales, with whom Princess Alice had been united in the bonds of the closest affection, especially since the Prince's illness, in which she had proved herself so devoted a nurse. The link between the Royal brother and sister is significantly shown by the fact that Princess Alice never visited England without paying long visits at Sandringham or at Marlborough House. The Prince of Wales was one of the chief mourners at the funeral in Darmstadt.

QUIET YEARS OF PUBLIC WORK 113

After this blow the Prince and Princess of Wales naturally

THE PRINCE IN 1879
From a Portrait by Angeli, published by Henry Graves and Co.

remained for some months in the deepest retirement. A new grief was, however, in store for them—the tragic death in the following

June of the young Prince Imperial, in whose career the Prince of Wales had always taken a warm and almost paternal interest. His Royal Highness was among the very first in this country to be informed of the terrible news, and he was of the greatest assistance to the stricken Empress Eugénie in making the complicated arrangements for the funeral. His active sympathy, and the announcement that the heir to the British Crown intended to be the principal pall-bearer of Napoleon III.'s ill-fated son, aroused much comment on the Continent, and gave great satisfaction to Frenchmen of all shades of political opinion. On a beautiful wreath of violets which was sent from Marlborough House for the funeral at Chislehurst were the words, written in the Princess of Wales's own hand :—

"A token of affection and regard for him who lived the most spotless of lives and died a soldier's death fighting for our cause in Zululand.
"From ALBERT EDWARD and ALEXANDRA,
July 12, 1879."

The Prince of Wales strongly supported the movement for erecting a memorial to the Prince Imperial in Westminster Abbey, and subscribed £130 to the fund which was raised for that object. The opposition to the scheme was, however, so strong that it fell to the ground. That the Prince's feelings were not modified in any way is shown by the fact that early in January 1883, His Royal Highness, accompanied by his two sons, Prince Albert Victor and Prince George, with the Duke of Edinburgh and the Duke of Cambridge, unveiled a monument to the Prince Imperial at Woolwich. This "United Service Memorial" was erected by a subscription raised throughout all ranks of the Army, Navy, Royal Marines, Militia, Yeomanry, and Volunteers, and Count Gleichen was the sculptor. The Prince of Wales, in a speech at the unveiling, commended the virtues, the blameless life, the courage, and obedience to orders manifested by the Prince, as a bright example to young men entering the Military Academy, and remarked that it was only a natural impulse which prompted his desire to join his English comrades in the war in South Africa, in which he fell fighting for the Queen of England.

QUIET YEARS OF PUBLIC WORK

In view of Princess Louise of Wales's subsequent marriage it is interesting to record that in the autumn of 1880 the Prince of Wales, accompanied by Prince Leopold and Prince John of Glucksburg, visited the Earl of Fife at Mar Lodge. On the evening of their arrival Lord Fife gave a grand ball, at which his distinguished visitors were present. The entertainment included a torchlight procession and dance by the Duff Highlanders. The party also enjoyed some deer-stalking in the Forest of Mar.

An incident worth recording occurred in January 1881, during a visit of the Prince and Princess of Wales to Normanton Park. Her Royal Highness drove with Lady Aveland to Oakham, and paid a visit to the ancient castle, on the inner walls of which are nailed numerous horse-shoes, the gift, or rather the toll, of various Royal and noble personages. A large horse-shoe of steel, perfect in shape and of elegant workmanship, had been made for the Princess to offer. Her Royal Highness examined the other horse-shoes in the Castle hall, and chose the position in which she desired her toll to be affixed, namely, over a large one supposed to have been the gift of Queen Elizabeth. The Princess greatly enjoyed following this ancient custom, a mark of territorial power possessed for many centuries by the Ferrers family, a shoe from the horse of every princely traveller who passed that way being a tax due to the Ferrers or Farriers. Among the horse-shoes specially noticed by the Princess of Wales were one contributed by the Queen when Princess Victoria, on 2nd September 1833; another by the Duchess of Kent on the same date; also one offered by the Prince Regent, afterwards George IV., on 7th January 1814.

It was in this year that the Prince of Wales had an opportunity of exhibiting in a public manner his strong interest in the British Colonies, the welfare of which was not then so much a matter of concern in the eyes of our statesmen as it is now. The occasion was a dinner given to the members of the Colonial Institute by the then Lord Mayor, Sir George MacArthur, himself an old colonist. An extraordinary number of distinguished men connected in various ways, official and other, with our colonies were present. In his speech the Prince of Wales pointed out that no function of the kind had ever taken place before—a statement which seems hardly credible nowadays, thanks in a great measure to His Royal Highness's own unwearied exertions in the interests of our colonial empire. The Prince also alluded to his Canadian tour, and took the opportunity of paying a graceful compliment to his friend Sir John Macdonald, who was present.

Very shortly after this dinner the Prince of Wales attended as patron the first meeting ever held in this country of the International Medical Congress.

The Prince of Wales was deeply grieved at the death of Dean Stanley, with whom, as we have seen, he had been on terms of close intimacy. At a meeting held in the Chapter-House of Westminster Abbey, His Royal Highness paid a touching and eloquent tribute to his dead friend's rare qualities, both of heart and intellect.

Generally speaking, this period of the Prince of Wales's life was not very eventful. His children were still quite young, and his public appearances, though tolerably frequent, did not usually possess more than a local importance. There were, however, some conspicuous exceptions, which broke the even current of the Prince's life. For example, it would be difficult to overestimate the value of the work which His Royal Highness did in promoting the International Fisheries Exhibition in 1883, which was visited by nearly three million people, and may be said to have been the first introduction into London of open-air entertainment on a large scale. Moreover, it resulted in a clear profit of £15,000, of which two-thirds was devoted to the relief of the orphan families of fishermen.

The success of the Fisheries suggested to the Prince the idea of another exhibition concerned with health and hygiene, which was held in 1884, and was nicknamed the "Healtheries." Not long before it was opened the Prince and Princess of Wales suffered a great bereavement in the death of the Duke of Albany, to whom the Prince had always been very much attached. He died quite suddenly in the south of France on 28th March, and the Prince of Wales instantly started for the Riviera and brought his brother's remains back to Windsor. In the following July, His Royal Highness, presiding at the festival of the Railway Guards' Friendly Society, took the opportunity of his first appearance at a public dinner to express in the name of the Queen and the Royal Family

QUIET YEARS OF PUBLIC WORK

their thanks for the public sympathy shown on the death of the Duke of Albany.

In August of this year was celebrated the jubilee of the abolition of slavery throughout the British dominions. The Prince of Wales attended a meeting at the Mansion-House and delivered a long and

THE PRINCE IN 1882

From the Painting by H. J. Brooks, published by Henry Graves and Co.

elaborate speech, evidently the result of much painstaking study, in which he reviewed the whole history of the anti-slavery movement.

The news of the fall of Khartoum came as a terrible shock to the Prince of Wales, who had long watched with increasing interest the career of General Gordon. Indeed, General Gordon had always been one of the Prince of Wales's great heroes, and it was chiefly owing to His Royal Highness's initiative that a fund was established for providing a national memorial to the hero of Khartoum. At the first meeting of the committee the Prince made a touching speech, in which he said of Gordon—

"His career as a soldier, as a philanthropist, and as a Christian is a matter of history. . . . Many would wish for some fine statue, some fine monument, but we who know what Gordon was feel convinced that were he living nothing would be more distasteful personally than that any memorial should be erected in the shape of a statue or of any great monument. His tastes were so simple and we all know he was anxious that his name should not be brought prominently before the public, though in every act of his life that name was brought, I am inclined to think, as prominently before the nation as that of any soldier or any great Englishman whom we know of at the present time."

It is well known that it was His Royal Highness's suggestion that a hospital and sanatorium should be founded in Egypt open to persons of all nationalities. The Princess was present at the special service held in St. Paul's on 13th March, the day of public mourning for the loss of General Gordon.

Three days later the Prince of Wales, accompanied by his eldest son, presided at a meeting of the Royal Colonial Institute, and spoke of the personal as well as of the political interest he took in everything that concerned the colonies. On the next day Prince Albert Victor was initiated as a Freemason in the presence of a large and most distinguished company, his father, the Prince of Wales, receiving the Royal apprentice in his quality of Worshipful Master of the Royal Alpha Lodge. On the following day the Prince of Wales, Prince Albert Victor, and the Duke of Edinburgh went to Berlin to congratulate the aged Emperor William on his 88th birthday.

It had been decided, not without the most anxious consideration, that the Prince and Princess of Wales, accompanied by their eldest son, should pay a visit to Ireland. The announcement was received with the greatest excitement both in Ireland and in America.

United Ireland, the chief organ of the Nationalist party, then edited by Mr. William O'Brien, and said to be largely written by Mr. T. M. Healy, brought out a special number devoted entirely to

VISIT TO IRELAND 119

expressions of opinion from eminent Irishmen of all kinds on the Prince's visit. Every Nationalist Member of Parliament, every

THE PRINCESS OF WALES IN HER ROBES AS DOCTOR OF MUSIC
From a Photograph by Chancellor, Dublin

prominent ecclesiastic, in a word, every Irishman of conspicuous Nationalist views, was invited to say what he thought of the forthcoming Royal visit. The answers filled a copious supplement, and their tenour was one of unanimous disapproval, expressed in some cases strongly, and in others in terms of studied moderation. Almost all the letters agreed in counselling an attitude of absolute indifference to the visit, but abstention from any kind of display of hostility to the Prince himself was insisted on ; and it was openly said that the part which His Royal Highness was playing in this pageant was a more or less passive one. This, perhaps, showed more than anything else that has occurred during the Prince's life the personal liking and respect in which he is held.

It may be added that when the Prince and Princess arrived early in April 1885 the Nationalist party made no sign, but as there was naturally a great display of rejoicing on the part of the Antinationalist citizens, the Press, perhaps unfortunately, chose to regard this reception as a proof that the Home Rulers were wholly discredited. The Nationalist leaders therefore made up their minds that it was necessary to make some protest against the Royal progress as an answer to these taunts, and accordingly from Mallow till the Royal party left Ireland they were the victims of some very unpleasing demonstrations, and at Cork collisions occurred between the police and the mob, though no serious injuries were reported on either side.

The Colonial and Indian Exhibition, called for short the "Colinderies," may be said to have been the most successful of all those with which the Prince of Wales was intimately associated. It was opened by the Queen on 4th May 1886, and Her Majesty was received by the Prince and Princess of Wales, His Royal Highness conducting her to the daïs. In the Royal Albert Hall, where the opening ceremony took place, everything was done to make the scene as impressive and interesting as possible ; and at the special desire of the Prince, Lord Tennyson wrote an Ode for the occasion, which was set to music by Sir Arthur Sullivan and sung by Madame Albani in the choir. This exhibition resulted in a net surplus of £35,000.

In September some correspondence between the Prince of Wales and the Lord Mayor, suggesting the establishment of a Colonial and Indian Institute to commemorate the Queen's Jubilee, was published, and excited a great deal of interest both at home and in the Colonies. A public subscription was opened at the Mansion-House ; and later in the same month His Royal Highness, having been informed that a movement was on foot to present him with a testimonial in recognition of his services in connection with the Colonial and Indian Exhibition, wrote to request that any fund subscribed might be devoted to the furtherance of the Imperial Institute, and a great deal of his time that autumn was dedicated to this scheme.

The Prince of Wales in 1886 also extended his patronage to two great engineering achievements, by opening the Mersey Tunnel and by laying the first stone of the Tower Bridge. It is interesting to note in this connection that the Prince has long been an honorary member of the Institution of Civil Engineers, and when he attended their annual dinner in the same year, he made an amusing speech, in which he attempted to picture what sort of a world ours would be without engineers.

One of the busiest years ever spent by the Prince and Princess of Wales was 1887, when the Queen's Jubilee was celebrated. To His Royal Highness was left the responsibility of a great number of the arrangements, and on him fell almost entirely the reception and entertainment of the foreign Royal personages who attended the splendid ceremony in the Abbey as the Queen's guests. In many cases the Prince was obliged to welcome in person the Royal visitor to London, and he was indefatigable in his efforts to make everything go off as smoothly and successfully as possible, while it need hardly be said that he took a very prominent part next to the Queen in all the Jubilee functions.

CHAPTER XI

SILVER WEDDING OF THE PRINCE AND PRINCESS OF WALES—
ENGAGEMENT AND MARRIAGE OF PRINCESS LOUISE OF WALES

CONSIDERABLE preparations were made early in 1888 for the Silver Wedding of the Prince and Princess of Wales, but it was well known that the Royal family were expecting daily to hear of the death of the old German Emperor, William I., which actually occurred just before the Prince and Princess of Wales's Silver Wedding Day, and everything in the way of public rejoicing was countermanded. Still the 10th of March was not allowed to pass entirely unobserved. The whole of the Royal family then in England, preceded by the Queen, called at Marlborough House to offer their congratulations in person, and for that one day the Court mourning was abandoned. The Prince and Princess of Wales with their family lunched at Buckingham Palace with the Queen, while in the evening Her Majesty attended a family dinner-party at Marlborough House, this being the first time she had ever been to dinner with the Prince and Princess in London. The Queen, after leaving Marlborough House, drove through some of the principal West End streets in order to see the illuminations. Her Majesty also gave a State ball at Buckingham Palace in honour of the event, and the King and Queen of Denmark gave a grand ball at the Amalienborg Palace at Copenhagen.

Archbishop Magee (then Bishop of Peterborough) writes in a letter to his intimate friend and biographer, Canon MacDonnell, the following amusing account of his share in the rejoicings:—

THE PRINCE'S SILVER WEDDING

"ATHENÆUM CLUB, 11th March 1888.

"Did you ever in your eminently respectable life dance on the tight rope? And did you ever do so in the presence of Royalty? No? Then I have beaten you.

"For I have this day performed that exceedingly difficult feat, and dead beat do I feel after it. I suppose you saw (for it was announced in all the papers) that H.R.H. was to worship at Whitehall with all his family, to keep his silver wedding, and that the Bishop of Peterborough was to preach. Not an easy thing to do, under any circumstances, to preach to Royalty in a pew opposite you, and also to a large middle-class congregation on a special occasion. But only think of having to add to this a special allusion to the late Emperor of Germany's death, and the present Emperor's condition, and all this within the space of forty minutes, the utmost length that it is considered good taste to inflict on H.R.H. Add to this that he specially requested an offertory for the Gordon Boys' Home, and of course implied some reference in the sermon to this. So that I had, within forty minutes, to preach a charity sermon, a wedding sermon, and a funeral one. Match me that if you can for difficulty. . . ."

In the unavoidable absence of the Bishop of London, Dean of the Chapels-Royal, the Archbishop of Canterbury was present, His Grace finally receiving the alms and giving the benediction. On the desk in the Royal Closet, in front of the Princess, was placed a beautiful bouquet of lilies of the valley, the emblem of the See and Province of Canterbury. The Princess quitted the chapel carrying the bouquet.

An enormous number of presents testified to the wide affection and respect in which the Royal couple were held. The Prince gave his wife a cross of diamonds and rubies, her favourite jewels; and from St. Petersburg, as a joint gift of the Emperor and Empress of Russia, came a superb necklace of the same gems composed of carefully selected stones. The five children of the Princess gave her a silver model of "Viva," her favourite mare. The Princess's eight bridesmaids, who were all alive and all married, gave the Royal bride of 1863 their autographs bound up in a silver book enshrined in a silver casket of Danish work.

The Freemasons of Great Britain presented Her Royal Highness with a very splendid diamond butterfly. The members of the Body-Guard were represented by a silver statue of a member of the corps, arrayed in the uniform originally designed by the Prince Consort. The Comte de Paris sent a large agate punch-bowl, studded with precious stones. Among the public gifts which afforded the Prince and Princess most pleasure was the Colonial Silver Wedding gift—a silver candelabrum adapted for electric light, and a fine twenty-one day movement clock to match. The Colonies became very enthusiastic over this gift, and more than £2000 was subscribed in small sums.

The King and Queen of Denmark gave a silver-gilt tea and coffee service; the Crown Prince and Princess of Denmark, a valuable vase of Danish china; the Empress Eugénie, a silver model of a two-masted ship of the time of Henry VIII.; and the King of the Belgians, a large silver tankard and a collection of the choicest exotics from the gardens at Laeken. The Austrian Ambassador presented an autograph letter from the Emperor Francis Joseph announcing that the Prince of Wales had been appointed to the Honorary Colonelcy of the 12th Hussar Regiment in the Austro-Hungarian Army. The French Ambassador was also received in audience and offered their Royal Highnesses an expression of good wishes on the part of the President of the French Republic and the French Government.

The presents received by the Prince and Princess were arranged in the Indian Room at Marlborough House. A prominent position was accorded to a gift from the Queen—a massive silver flagon of goodly height and proportions, the counterpart of one in the Kremlin. One corner of the Indian Room was filled with floral gifts, bouquets, wreaths, pyramids of lilies of the valley, and rich and rare exotics, sent by all classes of the community from all parts of the country and from the Continent.

In strong contrast to these rejoicings was the deep shadow thrown over the Prince of Wales and his family by the serious illness of the Emperor Frederick. All the arrangements of the Prince and Princess

ENGAGEMENT OF PRINCESS LOUISE

were naturally dependent on the news received almost hourly from the sick-chamber at Potsdam, but even in the midst of his terrible anxieties the Prince did not disappoint the loyal citizens of Glasgow, whose Exhibition he had promised to open, and who gave him a right Royal welcome. At length the long-dreaded blow fell. On 14th June the Emperor Frederick breathed his last after a reign of 99 days.

The following year was notable for the first break in the Prince's

THE DUCHESS OF FIFE AND THE PRINCESSES VICTORIA AND MAUD
From a Photograph by Lafayette

own family circle caused by marriage. But before the engagement of Princess Louise of Wales to the Earl of Fife was publicly announced, the Queen paid one of her necessarily rare visits to Sandringham, spending altogether four days there. While there Her Majesty witnessed a performance of *The Bells* and of *The Merchant of Venice*, given by Sir Henry Irving and the members of the Lyceum Company. The Prince's tenants presented an address of welcome to his Royal mother, to which Her Majesty gave the following gracious reply :—

"It has given me great pleasure to receive your loyal address, and I thank you sincerely for the terms in which you welcome me to Sandringham, and for the kind expressions which you have used towards the Prince and Princess of Wales. After the anxious time I spent here seventeen years ago, when, by the blessing of God, my dear son was spared to me and to the nation, it is indeed a pleasure to find myself here again, among cheerful homes and cheerful faces, and to see the kind feeling which exists between a good landlord and a good tenant; and I trust that this mutual attachment and esteem may long continue to make you happy and prosperous, and to strengthen, if possible, the affection of the Prince and Princess of Wales for the tenants of Sandringham."

Although Great Britain was not officially represented at the Paris Centennial Exhibition of this year, the Prince of Wales once more showed his friendship with France by going over with the Princess in semi-*incognito*. Their Royal Highnesses carefully inspected the whole Exhibition, paying special attention to the British section, and finished by ascending the Eiffel Tower.

Princess Louise's engagement was made public in the spring, and though it aroused almost as much surprise as satisfaction among the general public, yet those who were really in a position to know regarded it as the most natural thing in the world. Lord Fife had for years been admitted to the close intimacy of the Prince's family circle. His was the only bachelor's house at which the Princess of Wales had ever been entertained, he had long been a frequent and welcome guest at Sandringham, and when he took the oath and his seat in the House of Lords the Prince of Wales had paid him the rare honour of appearing as one of his introducers. Although rumours of the betrothal of the Prince's eldest daughter to various foreign Princes had for some time been rife, His Royal Highness had made no secret of the special importance which he attached to her marriage, for at that time it appeared by no means impossible that the Princess herself or her children might one day sit on the British throne. In these circumstances a foreign marriage of the particular kind which then seemed intrinsically probable would have been frankly unpopular with the British people, who would have pictured themselves as being perhaps one day reduced to

THE DUKE AND DUCHESS OF FIFE 127

bringing back their Queen, now wholly Germanised, from some obscure Grand Duchy.

The Prince of Wales on this occasion showed once more his intuitive sympathy with the feelings of his future subjects, for the news of the Royal engagement was received with an absolutely

THE DUKE OF FIFE
From a Photograph by the London Stereoscopic Co.

unforced outburst of popular enthusiasm, the more so when it became known that it was entirely a love match.

The Prince and Princess of Wales with their three daughters went to Windsor on 27th June and visited the Queen, when Her Majesty formally gave her consent to the engagement. On the receipt of the news at Marlborough House the fact was at once communicated to the Household, and the Marquis of Salisbury also was officially informed. The Earl of Fife was received by Her Majesty the same evening at Windsor Castle. In the House of Commons a Message from the Queen formally announced the intended marriage, and the First Lord of the Treasury gave notice of a motion to grant a suitable provision for the Royal bride, though owing to the great wealth of the bridegroom this was perhaps less necessary than it had been on the occasion of other Royal marriages.

The Earl of Fife (Alexander William George Duff), Baron Skene of Skene, Viscount Macduff, and Baron Braco of Kilbryde, County Cavan, was the only son of James, fifth Earl of Fife, and of the Countess of Fife, who was Lady Agnes Georgiana Elizabeth Hay, daughter of the Earl of Erroll. He was born on 10th November 1849, and was educated at Eton. He succeeded his father in the Scotch and Irish honours on 7th August 1879, and was created an Earl of the United Kingdom in 1885. He sat as Viscount Macduff in the House of Commons from 1874 to 1879 as Liberal member for Elgin and Nairn. Lord Fife, who is one of the largest landed proprietors in Scotland, owning extensive estates in Elgin, Banff, and Aberdeen, was created Duke of Fife and Marquis of Macduff in the peerage of the United Kingdom, on his wedding day, 27th July, having declined to take the title of Duke of Inverness.

The wedding was celebrated in the Chapel at Buckingham Palace, in the presence of the Queen, the Prince and Princess of Wales, with their sons and two younger daughters, the King of the Hellenes, the Crown Prince of Denmark, and the Grand Duke of Hesse.

The King of the Hellenes has always been one of the favourite brothers-in-law of the Prince of Wales, and His Royal Highness and the Princess went to Athens in the autumn to attend the wedding of the Duke of Sparta and Princess Sophie of Germany.

The following year was not very eventful. In March the Prince of Wales performed the ceremonies of finishing and opening the Forth Bridge in the presence of an illustrious assembly, including his son Prince George, the Duke of Edinburgh, who had travelled from Russia on purpose, the Duke of Fife, and the Earl of Rosebery, who was the host of their Royal Highnesses at Dalmeny. The last rivet, which the Prince fixed, is on the outside of the railway, and

THE FORTH BRIDGE

holds together three plates. Around its gilded top there runs a commemorative inscription. At the hour appointed for the formal declaration of the opening of the bridge, the wind was blowing so violently that it was impossible for His Royal Highness to make a speech. He simply said, " Ladies and Gentlemen, I now declare the Forth Bridge open."

It was in March, also, that the Prince of Wales and Prince George attended a Chapter of the Order of the Black Eagle in Berlin, at which Prince George was invested with the insignia of the Order. Subsequently their Royal Highnesses took part in the Ordensfest.

CHAPTER XII

THE BACCARAT CASE—BIRTH OF LADY ALEXANDRA DUFF—THE
PRINCE OF WALES'S FIFTIETH BIRTHDAY—ILLNESS OF PRINCE
GEORGE OF WALES

DURING the winter of 1890 various rumours had been rife as to a *cause célèbre* in which the Prince of Wales was to be called as a witness. These reports proved to have had substantial foundation in the following spring, when Sir William Gordon-Cumming, a cavalry officer of good family, who had distinguished himself in the Egyptian campaign, and was understood to enjoy the personal friendship of the Prince of Wales, brought an action for slander against five defendants—Mrs. Arthur Wilson, Mrs. A. S. Wilson, Mr. and Mrs. Lycett Green, and Mr. Berkeley Levett—who had accused him of cheating at baccarat at Tranby Croft, the Wilsons' place near Hull.

The trial opened early in June before Lord Chief Justice Coleridge, and the Prince of Wales was accommodated with a seat on the bench. The Court throughout wore the air of a theatre rather than of a Court of Justice, the bench and both the galleries being filled with ladies, who used their opera-glasses with freedom to discover the notabilities in Court, and to watch Sir William Gordon-Cumming under examination. The great counsel of the day were engaged. Sir Edward Clarke (Solicitor-General), with Mr. C. F. Gill as his junior, conducted the case for Sir William Gordon-Cumming ; and Sir Charles Russell (now Lord Chief Justice), with Mr. Asquith, appeared for the defendants, the Attorney-General having withdrawn from the case.

The Solicitor-General made a speech of singular power and

THE BACCARAT CASE

skill on behalf of his client. The point of the defence was that Sir William Gordon-Cumming—who was accused of the trick known as *la poussette*, by which a player at baccarat increases his stake after he sees that the cards are in his favour or the *coup* has been declared—had simply been playing on a system. This theory Sir William supported in the witness-box with great steadiness, and though his cross-examination was most severe, he maintained that on no occasion had he wrongfully increased the stake. When the cross-examiner came to a document which the plaintiff had signed, practically admitting his guilt, and which had been witnessed by the Prince of Wales, Sir William's explanation was, in effect, that he was hopeless of convincing those round him of his innocence, and that he desired for his own sake and that of others to avoid a scandal.

The Prince of Wales stepped into the box and was sworn in the ordinary way on the second day. Sir Edward Clarke addressed him as "Sir" and "Your Royal Highness," and Sir Charles Russell did the same. The Prince gave his evidence with much frankness, but it was largely of a formal character. His Royal Highness, however, said that at the time when, as banker, he questioned Sir William Gordon-Cumming on the largeness of his winnings, he did not think he had been cheating; but he added, in cross-examination by Sir Charles Russell, that in advising Sir William Gordon-Cumming to sign the document, he considered he had been acting most leniently.

As the Prince was leaving the witness-box an amusing incident occurred. A juryman rose from the back of the jury-box, and with *naïf* frankness put two important questions—whether the Prince had ever seen Sir William Gordon-Cumming cheating, and whether he believed him to be guilty. In reply to the first question the Prince answered that the banker would not be in a position to see foul play, and that among friends it would not be expected; and to the second he replied that, Sir William's accusers being so numerous, he could not but believe them. Having elicited these very important facts, the little juryman sat down, and the Prince stepped out of the box with a smile and a bow.

The Prince's evidence was followed by that of General Owen Williams, who, with Lord Coventry, drew up the document signed by the plaintiff. General Williams made two important statements —that he believed Sir William guilty, and that the Prince had objected to his placing his hands on the table in such a way that the counters could not properly be seen. In the course of the evidence it came out that the stakes played for on the two evenings were not large, but that Sir William won in all £225, which was paid him by cheque and which he retained.

The trial lasted seven days, and on 9th June the jury, after ten minutes' deliberation, returned a verdict for the defendants.

The most extraordinary interest was taken in the case, both in this country and on the Continent and in America, no doubt chiefly owing to the Prince of Wales's connection with it. A Prince of Wales has rarely been called as a witness in a case, although, of course, in the theory of English law, all men are equal, and the privileges, if any, which would attach to His Royal Highness would not attach to him in his capacity as Prince of Wales or Heir-Apparent to the Throne, but simply in his capacity as a peer of the United Kingdom.

It was pointed out by many that the conduct attributed to Sir William Gordon-Cumming was obviously not that of an officer and a gentleman, and in the House of Commons a week after the trial the Secretary of State for War expressed the regret of the Prince of Wales that he had not required Sir William to submit his case to the Commander-in-Chief.

The Prince of Wales became a grandfather for the first time this spring, for on 17th May the Duchess of Fife gave birth to a daughter at East Sheen Lodge. The question was immediately raised whether the infant should take Royal rank as a Princess of the Blood. When Sir William Beechey painted his portrait of Princess Victoria, the distance between the Duke of Kent's little daughter and the throne was as great as or even greater than that of the little daughter of the Princess Louise at her birth. It was ultimately settled, in accordance with the wishes, it was understood, of both the Prince of Wales and the Duke of Fife, that the infant should simply take the rank and precedence of a Duke's daughter and be called Lady Alexandra Duff.

The child was christened on 29th June in the Chapel-Royal, St. James's. The Queen came to London to act as sponsor to her great-

THE PRINCE'S FIFTIETH BIRTHDAY   133

granddaughter, and the Prince and Princess of Wales were joint sponsors for their grandchild. The Archbishop of Canterbury administered the rite of baptism. The Princess of Wales took the child from the nurse and placed her in the arms of the Queen, who gave the names of Alexandra Victoria Alberta Edwina Louise.

This autumn the Prince of Wales celebrated his fiftieth birthday, and it was computed that in his half-century of existence His Royal Highness must have been prayed for aloud in Anglican churches alone at least a hundred million times. The Prince's birthday is generally celebrated by him at home with his family, and he receives each year a large collection of interesting and valuable gifts from abroad. Few people are aware that the Prince of Wales and the Duc de Chartres were both born on the same day, the one in 1841 and the other in 1842. For many years it has been their custom to exchange presents on the 9th of each November. Occasionally that sent by His Royal Highness will be a peculiarly British gift, such as a fine rifle with all the latest improvements, the French Duke giving in return some valuable piece of French masculine jewellery, which one year took the form of a large gold cigar-case, superbly chased. The Princess of Wales and her daughters often give His Royal Highness a joint gift for his birthday. Among his valued treasures is a splendid album, each leaf of which is illuminated by a water-colour sketch by the Princess, the album being filled with photographs taken by the owner's three daughters. On the Prince's fiftieth birthday the theatrical managers of London presented a magnificent gold cigar-box, weighing 100 ounces, to His Royal Highness.

The month of December has been one of peculiar ill-omen to the Royal family, and it seemed as if December 1891 was to prove no exception. For the Princess of Wales and her daughters, who had been to Livadia on a visit to the Tsar, were recalled by the illness of Prince George of Wales, and the Prince and Princess went through some days of terrible anxiety. As soon as Prince George was declared to be suffering from enteric fever he was removed from Sandringham to London, and it was there that he was nursed. The illness evoked a remarkable degree of public sympathy, though perhaps the serious nature of the Prince's condition was hardly realised till all danger was practically over.

CHAPTER XIII

THE DUKE OF CLARENCE AND AVONDALE

THE year 1892 opened auspiciously both for the Royal family and the nation, inasmuch as, immediately on the convalescence of the Duke of York, the engagement of his elder brother, the Duke of Clarence and Avondale, to Princess Victoria Mary of Teck was announced. The projected alliance was received with every possible expression of popular approval. The public career of the Duke of Clarence, short as it had been, had already confirmed him in the public estimation as a worthy son of his father, who was known to have actively superintended the whole course of his education. A significant proof of the young Prince's amiability and unpretending modesty was to be found in the large number of personal friends whom he attached to himself, both at Cambridge and among his comrades of the 10th Hussars, by ties of sincere esteem. Moreover, it was generally known that between the Duke of Clarence and his mother there existed the strongest possible link of filial and maternal love, and so the Prince came to share in a measure the high place which the Princess of Wales has always held in the hearts of the British people.

The circumstances of the mournful event which threw a gloom over the whole winter of 1892 are still fresh in the memory of the nation. On 9th January the Duke of Clarence, who was spending the Christmas holidays with his parents at Sandringham, was attacked with influenza, having caught cold at the funeral of Prince Victor of Hohenlohe-Langenburg. Notwithstanding the devoted care lavished on him, his death occurred on the 14th, within a week of the day on which the tidings of his illness had first gone forth.

THE DUKE OF CLARENCE

From a Photograph by Chancellor, Dublin

Then, if ever, the Prince and Princess of Wales must have realised the respect and affection with which they are regarded by the British people. Their Royal Highnesses received the most touching letters from all over the world. One of those they most valued was from the Zulu chiefs at St. Helena. This was conveyed to the Prince through Miss Colenso, and ran as follows :—

"We have heard of the death of Prince Edward, the son of the Prince of Wales. We lament sincerely. Pray you present our lamentation to them all—to his grandmother, to his father and his mother, and his brother."

Their Royal Highnesses showed how deeply they appreciated the sympathy so spontaneously offered to them on every side by publishing the following Message :—

"WINDSOR CASTLE, 20*th January* 1892.

"The Prince and Princess of Wales are anxious to express to Her Majesty's subjects, whether in the United Kingdom, in the Colonies, or in India, the sense of their deep gratitude for the universal feeling of sympathy manifested towards them at a time when they are overwhelmed by the terrible calamity which they have sustained in the loss of their beloved eldest son. If sympathy at such a moment is of any avail, the remembrance that their grief has been shared by all classes will be a lasting consolation to their sorrowing hearts, and if possible will make them more than ever attached to their dear country."

On the Sunday following the death of the Duke, a private service was held in Sandringham Church, attended by the Prince and Princess, their daughters, Princess Victoria Mary of Teck, and Prince George. By the Prince of Wales's special wish his eldest son was given the simplest of military funerals, and the coffin was removed from Sandringham to Windsor on a gun-carriage, escorted by a number of the Prince's old comrades in arms. On the coffin lay the Prince's busby and a silken Union Jack, and even at Windsor, where among the impressive mass of mourners every Royal House was represented, everything was severely simple, and the pall-bearers were officers of the 10th Hussars.

The career of the Prince, so suddenly cut off ere he had well

THE DUKE OF CLARENCE AND AVONDALE 137

reached his prime, in addition to its historical interest, throws an instructive light upon the pains which the Prince of Wales has always expended on the education and training of his children. On none of his children did the Prince of Wales bestow more loving thought and care than on his eldest son, who was destined, as it then seemed, one day to bear all the anxieties and responsibilities of the British Crown.

The education of the young Prince was conceived and carried out upon a definite and well-considered plan. From childhood he was devotedly attached to his younger brother, Prince George, who warmly reciprocated his affection, and their father wisely determined that the two boys should not be separated, but should enter the Royal Navy together as cadets. This was done in June 1877, Prince Albert Victor being then thirteen and a half and Prince George being some seventeen months younger. From the very first the Prince of Wales caused it to be understood that his sons were to enjoy no privileges on account of their rank, but were to be treated exactly like their fellow-cadets on board the *Britannia*, and made to learn their profession just as if they had been the sons of an ordinary private gentleman. The young Princes spent two years in the *Britannia*, and both obtained a first-class in seamanship, entitling them to three months' sea-time, and for general good conduct they obtained another three months.

The Prince of Wales thoroughly realised the benefit he had himself derived from the travels which he had undertaken as a youth, and therefore he arranged that his sons should spend three years in making a tour round the world, that their minds might be equipped by experience of men and cities, and that they might acquire an abiding impression of the extent and resources of the British Empire. Accordingly, the young Princes started in the *Bacchante*, being entrusted to the care of the Rev. J. N. Dalton, now Canon of Windsor. The Princes kept careful diaries, and on their return they published a most interesting and detailed account of their experiences. In the *Bacchante*, just as in the *Britannia*, they were treated exactly like other officers of their age and standing, except that they had a private cabin under the poop. They joined the gun-room mess, the members of which were granted a special allowance—an arrangement which had before been made when the Duke of Edinburgh began his naval career.

On the return of the Princes from their tour it became at last necessary to separate them. Prince George, as the younger son, might be left to continue his career in the noble service to which he had become devoted, but his elder brother, being in the immediate succession to the Throne, must, it was felt, be associated, as his father had been before him, with other walks of national life as well.

Accordingly, in 1883, the Prince of Wales accompanied Prince Albert Victor to Cambridge and saw him matriculated as an undergraduate member of Trinity College, that ancient and splendid foundation to which he himself belonged. It was at Cambridge that certain sterling qualities possessed by Prince Albert Victor first became manifest to any considerable circle, and through them to the public at large. His life at the University was simple and well ordered. He had not—nor was it desirable that he should have—the specialised intellect which wins University prizes and scholarships, but he displayed in a marked degree that peculiarly Royal quality of recognising intellect in others. Of those whom he admitted to his friendship while at Cambridge nearly all have become, or are becoming, distinguished in various walks of life. It must not be supposed that the Prince was idle at the University. On the contrary, he read for six or seven hours a day regularly—a good deal more than the average undergraduate can be persuaded to do—and he was in another respect intellectually ahead of most of his contemporaries, namely, in his familiar knowledge of modern languages. He had read German at Heidelberg with Professor Ihne, and he kept it up while at Cambridge with a German tutor. He spoke French easily and well, and he had also a literary knowledge of that language, having spent some time in Switzerland with a French tutor.

Prince Albert Victor strongly resembled his father in many respects, notably in his habits of order and method, and in his complete freedom from affectation or assumption. He was, indeed, if anything, almost too modest and retiring, but those who knew him bore witness to his real geniality and thoughtful consideration for others. At Cambridge he attended his College chapel twice on

THE PRINCESS OF WALES

From a Photograph by Gave and Stuart

Sundays, and once or twice during the week. He generally dined in the College hall, when he would be assigned a place at the Fellows' table. He was fond, however, of giving little dinner-parties of six or eight in his own rooms in College, usually on Thursdays, his guests on these occasions often including some of the senior members of the University. After dinner, the Royal host would generally arrange a rubber or two of whist. He did not take part in cricket or football, but was fond of polo and hockey, and he occasionally hunted. He might often have been met in the neighbourhood of Cambridge riding in the company of a few of his undergraduate friends, to whom he liked to offer a mount, especially in cases where he knew it was needed. The Prince had an inherited love of music, and he attended pretty regularly some weekly concerts of chamber music given at the Cambridge Town Hall. One traditionally Royal quality the Prince possessed in an extraordinary degree, namely, a perfectly marvellous memory for names and faces. Indeed, his memory in general was singularly tenacious, and in his historical studies he exhibited a wonderful power of quickly mastering the most intricate genealogical tables.

The Prince came of age in 1885, and the house-party at Sandringham given to celebrate the occasion was one of the largest gatherings ever held there. The company included a considerable number of Prince Albert Victor's Cambridge friends.

On the conclusion of Prince Albert Victor's residence at Cambridge, the honorary degree of LL.D. was conferred upon him, and then the Prince of Wales decided that it was time for his elder son to enter the army. He was accordingly gazetted a lieutenant in the 10th Hussars, of which the Prince of Wales is colonel, and while he was quartered at Aldershot the father and son saw a great deal of each other. In the army, as in the navy, Prince Albert Victor was treated as far as possible exactly like his brother officers; and indeed it is highly probable that, had he been offered any exceptional privileges, he would have steadily refused to take advantage of them. The Prince became a captain in the 9th Lancers and in the 3rd King's Royal Rifles and aide-de-camp to the Queen in 1887, and two years later attained the rank of major, returning to his old regiment, the 10th Hussars.

THE DUKE OF CLARENCE AND AVONDALE 141

The Prince of Wales retained such pleasant recollections of his own visit to India, that he determined that his elder son should at an early date make a tour in the Queen's great Eastern dependency. The tour was arranged, and proved extremely successful from every point of view. Prince Albert Victor was gazetted honorary colonel of the 4th Bengal Infantry, the 1st Punjab Cavalry (Prince Albert Victor's Own), and the 4th Bombay Cavalry.

Soon after his return from India, Prince Albert Victor was created Duke of Clarence and Avondale, and Earl of Athlone, in the peerage of the United Kingdom. He was formally introduced to the House of Lords by his father on 23rd January 1890, the ceremony being watched by the Princess of Wales from a gallery. This was an event unique in English history. The Duke of Clarence was the only eldest son of a Prince of Wales who attained his majority, to say nothing of taking his seat in the House of Lords, while his father was still Heir-Apparent to the Crown.

During the year which followed, the Prince of Wales gave up regularly a certain portion of his time to initiating his elder son in all the varied, if monotonous, duties which were likely to fall to his lot, a task which was really in no wise irksome, for those who knew the Duke of Clarence best were well aware that his father had ever been his best friend, and that he himself was never so happy as when he was allowed to share in any sense his father's life and interests.

CHAPTER XIV

1893-1897

AFTER the death of the Duke of Clarence the Prince of Wales and his family naturally retired into the deepest privacy, and it was many months before His Royal Highness had sufficiently recovered from the blow to be able to take up again the thread of his public duties.

The year 1893, however, brought to the Prince a very fortunate distraction, which prevented his mind from dwelling too much on his bereavement in a way that could not have been accomplished by the customary round of ceremonial visits and functions. This distraction was His Royal Highness's appointment as a member of the Royal Commission on the Housing of the Poor. The Prince was genuinely delighted with this opportunity. He threw himself with the greatest zeal into the work, and not only attended all the sittings, which took place in one of the House of Lords' Committee Rooms, but visited, *incognito*, some of the very poorest quarters of London. It is well known that he was exceedingly anxious to serve on the Labour Commission, but Her Majesty's Ministers have always been unwilling that the Heir-Apparent should take an active part in matters connected, even indirectly, with politics, and he has had therefore constantly to play the part of the Queen's deputy without the responsibilities and interests naturally attaching to the position.

It is no exaggeration to say that there are few men now living who possess better general qualifications for the difficult work of serving on Royal Commissions than the Prince of Wales. He is familiar with an almost bewildering variety of subjects, and possesses a wonderful faculty for almost instinctively grasping the important features and the really essential points of any matter under discussion.

THE PRINCE AND PRINCESS OF WALES, WITH THE DUCHESS OF FIFE AND
LADY ALEXANDRA DUFF

From a Photograph by Gunn and Stuart

He is a model chairman of a committee, and, though he cannot ever display the slightest trace of personal or party feeling, it is well known that he follows with intense interest all the political and social movements of the day, and it is no secret that he is thoroughly an Imperialist.

The Prince's work on the Housing of the Poor Commission was particularly congenial to him, for he has always shown an unaffected interest in the working-classes. He has long been an annual subscriber to the Working-Men's Club and Institute Union, and is a generous donor to the Working-Men's College. On one occasion His Royal Highness was accidentally informed that an exhibition promoted by the working-men in South London was somewhat languishing for lack of sufficient notice, and unofficially the Prince arranged to visit the exhibition. He went through it carefully, buying and paying for such articles as took his fancy, and the moment the fact became known the promoters had no reason to complain of neglect on the part of the general public, who were eager to see what had interested the Prince of Wales.

Throughout the year 1893 the Prince of Wales was busily employed in various ways. In March he paid a formal visit to the Public Record Office to inspect some of the priceless national manuscripts deposited there, and in May he had the satisfaction of seeing that great enterprise which he had himself originated, the Imperial Institute, inaugurated in State by his Royal Mother. It was at the Institute that Mr. Gladstone was hissed by some unmannerly persons, to the great annoyance of the Prince, who has never concealed the strong respect and esteem in which he holds both Mr. and Mrs. Gladstone.

It is interesting also to record that in March of this year the Princess of Wales, who was accompanied by the Duke of York, was received by the Pope in private audience. The interview lasted about an hour.

The official announcement was made in May of the betrothal of the Duke of York and Princess May of Teck. On 6th July, after a very short engagement, the marriage took place in the Chapel-Royal, St. James's, in the presence of all the Royal family, as well as the present Emperor of Russia and the King and Queen of Denmark. The

1893–1897 145

Prince of Wales naturally took a prominent part in supervising all the arrangements, and was much gratified by the outburst of popular

THE QUEEN AND THE DUKE AND DUCHESS OF YORK
From a Photograph by Hughes and Mullins, Ryde

enthusiasm which greeted his son's union with the daughter of the universally-beloved Duchess of Teck.

It is interesting to note how frequently, ever since the marriage, the Prince of Wales has associated the Duke of York with himself in the performance of his public duties, while the constant companionship of father and son, both in Norfolk and in London, is a striking testimony to their complete sympathy with one another.

The following year was notable for two Royal marriages in the Prince of Wales's immediate circle, and for a bereavement which touched both the Prince and Princess in their closest family affections. His Royal Highness went to Coburg in April to be present at the wedding of his niece, Princess Victoria Melita of Saxe-Coburg and Gotha, and his nephew, the Grand Duke of Hesse, the only son of the lamented Princess Alice. The occasion brought together a remarkable number of prominent members of Royal Houses, including the Queen and the German Emperor, and was rendered additionally memorable by the fact that the engagement of the present Tsar of Russia to the bridegroom's sister was then publicly announced.

The Prince of Wales, who was on this occasion accompanied by the Princess, went to St. Petersburg in August for the wedding of the Grand Duchess Xenia, which was celebrated with all the lavish magnificence of Russian Court ceremonies.

Although the Tsar was not then in his usual robust health, there was nothing to indicate how soon the Prince and Princess of Wales were to be recalled to Russia on a far different mission. To their lasting sorrow, the summons to the Tsar's death-bed at Livadia arrived too late for them to be present at the last. Their Royal Highnesses left London on 31st October, immediately on receipt of an urgent message from the Tsaritsa, and had proceeded as far as Vienna when the news was broken to them that all was over. They, however, continued their melancholy journey, which was much delayed by bad weather, in order that they might be with the widowed Empress and her son through the terrible strain of the return to St. Petersburg, and the ordeal of the funeral ceremonies.

The Prince of Wales's fifty-third birthday was spent at Livadia, and for the first time since his birth the anniversary celebrations in London and at Sandringham did not take place.

When the funeral *cortége* reached St. Petersburg, the Duke of

York joined his parents, and together they attended the elaborate obsequies of the Emperor, and the very quiet wedding of the young Tsar and Princess Alix of Hesse, which followed a few days later. The Prince of Wales remained in Russia for the Princess's birthday, and left with the Duke of York the following day, while Her Royal Highness stayed behind to support her sister, the Empress Alexander.

The relations between England and Russia after the Prince's return became noticeably more cordial, and there is no doubt that this was owing in a large measure to His Royal Highness's personal exertions, and the sympathy which he and his son displayed with the Russian people in their great sorrow.

During this year of 1894 the Prince of Wales exhibited his usual complaisance in attending various local ceremonies. Among these may be mentioned the opening of the Tower Bridge by the Prince and Princess, on behalf of the Queen, in June; while in July their Royal Highnesses attended the Welsh Eisteddfod at Carnarvon, where they were received with great enthusiasm. A special session was held, at which the Prince of Wales was initiated as "Iorweth Dywysog" (Edward the Prince), the Princess of Wales as "Hoffder Prydain" (Britain's Delight), and the Princess Victoria of Wales as "Buddug" (the modern Welsh form of Boadicea).

The Prince of Wales is always willing to emphasise his connection with the Principality from which he takes his title, and when the long-desired University of Wales became an accomplished fact, he readily consented to be its first Chancellor. His Royal Highness was installed in this office at Aberystwith in June 1896, and his first act as Chancellor was to confer an honorary degree on the Princess. At the luncheon which followed, the Prince's health was proposed by Mr. Gladstone.

In the following month, the marriage of Princess Maud of Wales to Prince Charles of Denmark took place in the chapel of Buckingham Palace in the presence of the Queen and the Royal families of the two countries.

The Prince of Wales, for a variety of reasons, took a much greater part in the Jubilee festivities of 1897 than he did in those of ten years before. All the arrangements were submitted for his approval as well as the Queen's, and it was largely owing to his conspicuous organising ability that everything went off with such triumphant success. Both the Prince and Princess associated themselves in a special manner with the occasion, the former by his

THE PRINCE IN ADMIRAL'S UNDRESS UNIFORM
From a Photograph taken in 1897 by Mullins, Ryde

Hospital Fund for London, and the latter by her thoughtful scheme of providing one good dinner for the very poorest. The Hospital Fund greatly benefited by the sale of a special stamp, the design of which was selected by the Prince himself.

The Prince of Wales, who is an Admiral of the Fleet, represented the Queen at the magnificent naval review at Spithead, which was generally agreed to be, in its way, the finest spectacle of all that the Jubilee festivities afforded. Many foreign warships were sent by other countries as tokens of international courtesy. Towards the officers of these vessels the Prince of Wales displayed all his wonted cordiality ; and in the arrangements for their entertainment his efforts were heartily seconded by Mr. Goschen, the First Lord of the Admiralty, and the other naval authorities. The spectacle of so vast a concourse of British vessels was rendered doubly impressive by the knowledge that it had been assembled without weakening in the slightest degree the squadrons on the numerous British naval stations all over the world. There was much point in the remark said to have been made by the United States Special Ambassador to Mr. Goschen : "I guess, sir, this makes for peace!"

On the eventful morning of the 22nd June, when the Jubilee honours were announced, it was found that the Queen, while conferring some mark of her favour on each of her sons, had created a new and special dignity for the Prince of Wales. The announcement was made in the following terms :—

"The Queen has been graciously pleased, on the occasion of Her Majesty's Diamond Jubilee, to appoint Field-Marshal His Royal Highness the Prince of Wales, K.G., G.C.B., to be Great Master and Principal Knight Grand Cross of the Most Honourable Order of the Bath."

That this distinction was very gratifying to His Royal Highness was significantly shown in the following month, when he gave a great banquet at St. James's Palace to the Knights Grand Cross of the Order of the Bath in celebration of his appointment. It was an absolutely unique gathering of men who had rendered distinguished service to the State, in statesmanship, in diplomacy, in the profession of arms, in the navy, and in the departments of civil administration.

The rest of the Diamond Jubilee year was spent in comparative quietude by the Prince and Princess of Wales, although His Royal Highness took an active part in the exceptionally brilliant season. He attended, among other great functions, the Fancy Dress Ball given by the Duchess of Devonshire, wearing on this occasion the splendid costume of the Grand Master of the Knights-Hospitallers of Malta.

During the summer the Prince made a sojourn at Marienbad, deserting Homburg for the first time for some years.

THE PRINCE AS GRAND MASTER OF THE KNIGHTS-HOSPITALLERS OF MALTA,
AT THE DUCHESS OF DEVONSHIRE'S BALL

From a Photograph by Lafayette

This summer was also rendered memorable for the visit paid by the Duke and Duchess of York to Ireland. Their Royal Highnesses spent a fortnight there, stopping with the Lord-Lieutenant, Earl Cadogan, in Dublin; afterwards visiting some of the great houses of the Irish nobility, and seeing a great deal of the lovely scenery for which Ireland is famous, including Killarney, from which the Duke of York takes the title of Baron.

THE DUKE OF YORK IN HIS ROBES AS A KNIGHT OF ST. PATRICK
From a Photograph by Lafayette

In Dublin the Duke of York and the ever-popular Lord Roberts were installed with great pomp and ceremony as Knights of the Order of St. Patrick. The Duke wore the same sword which his father had used when he was installed some three-and-twenty years before.

152   THE PRINCE OF WALES

This Royal visit to Ireland exhibited in a striking manner the extent to which party passions had been allayed in the distressful country. The Duke and Duchess of York had everywhere a

THE DUCHESS OF YORK
From a Photograph by Chancellor, Dublin

respectful and frequently an enthusiastic reception; and in almost every address received by their Royal Highnesses the desirability of establishing a Royal residence in Ireland was pointedly referred to.

The profound effect of the visit was seen a month or two later, when, on the death of the lamented Duchess of Teck, the Lord Mayor and Lady Mayoress of Dublin telegraphed their condolences, both officially and privately, not to the Duke of Teck, as might have been expected, but to the Duke and Duchess of York. On this mournful occasion, also, the Corporation of "rebel" Cork passed a resolution of sympathy.

As has been so singularly often the case, the autumn brought yet another bereavement to the Royal family in the entirely unexpected death of Princess Mary, Duchess of Teck. The Princess, who stood in the relation of second cousin to the Prince of Wales, was, although belonging technically to the same generation as the Queen, but a few years older than His Royal Highness, and the most affectionate and close relations had always existed between them, a fact shown on many occasions throughout their joint lives, and nowhere more strikingly than in the great satisfaction expressed by both the Prince and Princess of Wales at the marriage of their only surviving son to the daughter of the Duke and Duchess of Teck.

Earlier in the autumn an attempt was made to use the Prince of Wales's great personal prestige and popularity in order to bring to a close the struggle between masters and men in the engineering trade. The writer received the following reply :—

"MARLBOROUGH HOUSE, PALL MALL, S.W.,
8th October 1897.

"DEAR SIR—I am directed by the Prince of Wales to acknowledge the receipt of your letter of the 4th inst., and to inform you, in reply, that, while he deeply deplores the disastrous state of affairs in the engineering industry, he feels that it would not be right or proper for him to attempt in any way to interfere or to mix himself up in them. His Royal Highness regrets that he is unable to act on your suggestion.—I am, Sir, your obedient servant,

"FRANCIS KNOLLYS."

THE NORWICH GATE AT SANDRINGHAM
Photograph by Ralph, Dersingham

CHAPTER XV

SANDRINGHAM

WHEN the Prince of Wales was about to set up a separate establishment, the Queen and the Prince Consort instructed some of their most trusted friends to look out for a suitable country estate for the Heir-Apparent. At one moment it was proposed to buy Newstead Abbey, but its Byronic associations caused it to be purchased as soon as it came into the market. Eynsham, in Oxfordshire, an estate belonging to Lord Macclesfield, also came under consideration, as also Elveden, in Suffolk, and Hatherop, in Gloucestershire. Lord Palmerston seems to have suggested Sandringham, which at that time belonged to his stepson, Mr. Spencer Cowper, and accordingly the Norfolk estate was bought for £220,000.

The estate consisted of eight thousand acres, the nominal rental being about £7000 a year, but everything about Sandringham was at that time in very bad order. The house was small and dilapidated,

SANDRINGHAM

and the shooting and outlying portions of the estate had been utterly neglected. It is said that the whole rental has been expended on the property during the last thirty-five years, and a very considerable sum has also been spent on the new house, the new gardens, the park, and the home farms. Every kind of improvement has been carried out, gradually but steadily, and now it may be considered a model estate from every point of view. One of the first institutions set up by His Royal Highness was an admirable village club, entirely built at the Prince's own expense. The regulations enforced are based on what is called Dr. Arnold's system, and give the *maximum* of freedom to the members.

On one occasion, when speaking of himself at a meeting of the Royal Benevolent Institution, His Royal Highness said, " I think I may style myself a colleague of many of you present as a farmer on a small scale, and I only hope that I may never have occasion to be a pensioner of this institution. It is impossible for any British gentleman to live at his country place without taking an interest in agriculture, and in all those things which concern the farmers of this great country."

The Prince has always been a very keen competitor at the various national and local shows, and he takes his duties as President of the Royal Agricultural Society very seriously. All the Norfolk shows, from the flower show to the poultry show, are patronised by both their Royal Highnesses ; and in this, as in so many other matters, the Squire of Sandringham sets an excellent example to those round him. The Allotments Act was practically anticipated by the Prince of Wales at Sandringham. Indeed the tenants of His Royal Highness are well aware that he interprets very generously any Act telling in their favour.

The old mansion, which was small and inconvenient, was pulled down, and the present house was erected on a more suitable site, from the designs of Mr. Humbert. The work was not completed till 1871. The new mansion is a very pretty gabled building, and though commodious enough for the Prince's requirements, it will not compare in point of size with many of the "stately homes of England." On the inner wall of the vestibule, above the hall door, is set a tablet bearing, in Old English characters, the inscription : " This house was built by Albert Edward, Prince of Wales, and Alexandra, his wife, in the year of Our Lord, 1870."

The Royal host and hostess, as well as their family and their guests, spend much of their time in the great hall, a really beautiful apartment, with a lofty ceiling of open oak work. Many family souvenirs are gathered here, including a fine painting of the Princess of Wales's birthplace, portraits of the King and Queen of Denmark, two miniature cannon, which were given by Napoleon III. to the Prince of Wales and to his sister, the Princess Royal, and a number

THE EAST FRONT, SANDRINGHAM

Photograph by Ralph, Dersingham

of family portraits and photographs. Facing the main entrance is the head of a wild bull, belonging to the famous Chillingham herd, which was shot by the Prince in 1872. Underneath are Sir Walter Scott's lines :—

> Fierce on the hunter's quiver'd band
> He rolls his eyes of swarthy glow,
> Spurns with black hoof and horn the sand,
> And tosses high his mane of snow.

To those who study the Prince of Wales's personal nature and character, no apartment in Sandringham can be more interesting than the library, or rather that section of the libraries, for

SANDRINGHAM 157

there are three, which is the special concern of His Royal Highness. The fittings are those of the cabins used by the Prince on board the *Serapis* during his voyage to and from India. The blotting-books and the tables and chairs are all covered in dark blue or green leather, and on each the Prince's plumes and monogram are stamped in gold. A glance at the shelves shows what are our future King's literary tastes and preferences. He is evidently intensely interested in the history of his own country, especially what may be called the history of our own time. Several shelves are entirely devoted to works dealing with the Indian Mutiny, including the official reports, memoirs, histories, and even novels. The Prince always buys every new work connected with the public or private administration of the Queen's Eastern Empire. Special attention has also evidently been paid to the Crimean War, and the Prince possesses a unique collection of Colonial histories and documents. But most of the standard works of reference are to be found in the first library, a fine apartment, often used as a writing-room and reading-room by visitors.

The second library is really the Equerries' room. It is there the Gentlemen of the Household are often to be found. Here are collected together the French and English works of reference and classics, and a unique collection of county histories. Novels and memoirs are not neglected, and no week passes, when the Prince and Princess are in residence, without a large consignment of British and foreign books finding its way to Sandringham.

Another room which is much used by His Royal Highness is the smoking-room. There each day are placed all the newspapers, including files of most of the leading dailies. In this room are preserved many splendid cigar-cases and tobacco-boxes presented to the Prince at various times by his friends and relations. Some of them are veritable works of art. As is well known, the Prince of Wales has always been a smoker. His brother-in-law, the late Tsar of Russia, always sent His Royal Highness each Christmas a cabinet of cigars, and the Emperor of Austria is represented by a case of Havanas of various sizes and qualities. These gifts are placed, immediately on their arrival, in a special room, which is kept at an even temperature all the year round.

The Prince has a very remarkable collection of silver cigar-lighters, but these are kept at Marlborough House. A stock of the Prince's own special tobacco is kept at the Marlborough Club, at the Jockey Club Rooms at Newmarket, at the Royal Yacht Squadron Club-House, and on board all the Royal yachts. He is always willing to share his exceptionally good stock of cigars with those with whom he is brought in contact. On one occasion, when attending a big fire, His Royal Highness asked a reporter for some

SANDRINGHAM FROM THE GROUNDS
Photograph by Ralph, Dersingham

details, which were instantly given. At the conclusion of the conversation, the Prince offered his informant a cigar, which the latter immediately wrapped up in a page of his note-book and placed in his pocket. "Don't you smoke?" asked the Prince. "Oh yes," said the reporter; "but I am not likely ever to get another cigar from the Prince of Wales." The Prince laughed, and once more producing his cigar-case said, "You had better have another one, this time to smoke."

SANDRINGHAM

The Prince of Wales transacts much of the business connected with the Sandringham estate in a pleasant morning-room. There he receives at stated times the bailiffs and others concerned in the management of the estate, and, as he farms himself over 1000 acres, he has much to do in the way of supervision.

Sandringham can boast of one of the finest private billiard-rooms in England, and it is one of the very few country-houses where there are bowling alleys. The Prince and his children are very fond of the old-fashioned English game of bowls.

In 1891 the entire roofing of the main building of Sandringham House, together with all the rooms and their contents on the two upper floors, was destroyed by fire. The bells of the various churches in the district clashed out the alarm. Gangs of men and women speedily set to work to clear the principal lower rooms of their furniture and rare, valuable, and interesting contents. The Princess of Wales was stopping with the Empress of Russia, the Prince was also away at the time. The amount of damage done was about £15,000. That portion of the house which was destroyed has been rebuilt in a thoroughly fire-proof fashion, with iron and concrete floors and roofs ; and the opportunity was taken of making many additions to various portions of the house, in fact, about eighteen rooms were added. It was very characteristic of the Prince of Wales that, by his orders, the general works were all carried out by local tradesmen.

One of the most interesting departments of Sandringham Hall is the stables, which contain a great number of carriages. There are Russian sledges, only used in the coldest weather ; a Hungarian snow-carriage, lined with rose colour ; Norwegian carioles ; a smart American buggy, painted bright yellow ; a truly beautiful gold inlaid jinricksha, sent to His Royal Highness from Japan, which is for show rather than for use ; a char-à-banc, presented by the late Duke of Sutherland to the Prince ; and, it need hardly be said, every kind of ordinary two- and four-wheeled vehicle now in general use, from the modest Norfolk cart to the stately landau ; while by the big coach is to be seen the charming miniature four-in-hand presented by His Royal Highness to the Princess just before his departure for India.

Both the Prince and Princess are passionately fond of horses, and Her Royal Highness pays a daily visit to her pony-stable, which was built in 1874 for her four French ponies, now replaced by equally valuable animals of British extraction. Bina, Merry-Antics, Bow, and Bell are the fortunate occupants of this model pony-stable, which is considered the prettiest building of the kind in the world, the walls being lined with white tiles, picked out in green glazed bricks, finished at the top by a green-tiled frieze and an open wooden roof. Above each manger is written in gold letters the

THE PRINCESS'S DAIRY AT SANDRINGHAM
Photograph by Ralph, Dersingham

name of the pony which occupies the stall. The Princess at one time was very fond of driving tandem, and she has one of the best tandem teams in Great Britain.

But the Princess does not only confine her attention to ponies; she is very fond of bay horses, and possesses a pair of the famous greys bred in the Imperial stables at Leipzig. For many years Her Royal Highness always rode Kinsky, a Hungarian horse; and she was said to be one of the best horsewomen in Norfolk.

The saddle-room is not the least fascinating portion of the stable-yard. Much of the harness is silver and gold-plated. The Princess has always preferred brown harness to black, and all that used by her is made in tan leather, with brass mounts.

SANDRINGHAM

There are a number of interesting photographs and paintings, including a picture in oils of a very beautiful chestnut mare, Victoria, long ridden by the Princess, and given to her when she was a bride by the Queen. Below this portrait of a departed favourite is one of her hoofs mounted in silver, with the name of the owner written across. There are some valuable prints of celebrated trainers and jockeys, with some of the latter's whips, spurs, and caps. A

THE KENNELS, SANDRINGHAM

Photograph by T. Fall, Baker Street, W.

"Vanity Fair" cartoon of the Prince, surrounded by a number of his friends at Newmarket, is also given a prominent place in the Sandringham saddle-room ; and not the least interesting memento now there is Mr. John Porter's silver-wedding gift to his Royal patrons. In a silver frame, surmounted by the Prince of Wales's feathers, is a white velvet tablet with the name "Ormonde" woven from the famous race-horse's hair. The border contains pieces of the hair of thirty-three famous winners, the name of each being in silver letters beneath. Close by is to be seen the racing-saddle generally used by Fred Archer.

M

162 THE PRINCE OF WALES

Parallel with the stables runs the building known as the kennels. At one time, in the paddock between the stables and the kennels, there was a bear-pit, but the occupant thereof was sent to the Zoo after the Prince's valued head-keeper, Mr. Jackson, had been hunted by Bruin just when he was about to feed him with some peculiarly

THE PRINCESS WITH HER FAVOURITE DOGS
Photograph by T. Fall, Baker Street, W.

bearish delicacy. This corner of Sandringham is by no means confined to horses and dogs. Here also are kept some of the Princess's pet cats; a number of doves descended from the single pair presented to Her Royal Highness during her first visit to Ireland; her Australian pigeons, quite unlike the more humble home variety; a Barbary dove belonging to the Duchess of York; and some very

SANDRINGHAM 163

fine water-fowl, to say nothing of Cockie, the Princess of Wales's cockatoo, who is said to be over a hundred years old.

The kennels are, in their way, quite as fine as the stables. They are very cleverly arranged, all fitted with hot-water pipes, and admirably ventilated. The dogs are exercised in the park, in three paddocks in front of the kennels, or in a large yard paved with red, blue, and brick tiles. All the food consumed in the kennels comes from special kitchens attached to the building. There is also a dog hospital and a nursery, always occupied by one or more litters.

The Prince and Princess are both keen dog-fanciers, and they possess some of the very finest animals in the world. They both exhibit at the leading shows, and Her Royal Highness is the Patron of the Ladies' Kennel Association.

MARLBOROUGH HOUSE FROM THE SOUTH-WEST
Photograph by Ralph, Dersingham

CHAPTER XVI

LIFE IN LONDON

ALTHOUGH Marlborough House is not in so real a sense the "home" of the Prince of Wales and his family as Sandringham is, His Royal Highness is obliged by his position to spend so much of every year in London that the beautiful old Georgian house has become the centre of his social, philanthropic, and official life.

Surprise has sometimes been expressed that the Prince of Wales has not long ago moved to one of the larger, and one would think more commodious, Royal residences in London, such as Buckingham, Kensington, or St. James's Palaces. But both their Royal Highnesses have so many associations, both of joy and sorrow, with Marlborough House, that they have preferred to remain there, in spite of its comparatively unpretending character. There is scarcely an object in the house which does not remind the Prince and Princess of some happy incident of their joint lives. The very carpet which is down in the drawing-room was presented to them on the occasion of their wedding ; and the Prince's great interest in everything that concerns the history of the country and of the Empire is strikingly shown in each of his homes, for the rooms of both Marlborough House and Sandringham are lined with fine paintings and engravings recalling great events of the Victorian era.

Although Marlborough House is the official residence of the Heir-Apparent, it is considered a private house for taxation purposes, and the Prince pays over £1000 a year in rates to St. Martin's parish.

His Royal Highness's study at Marlborough House, where none but his intimates are admitted, looks like the room of a hard-working man of business. He works at an old-fashioned pedestal desk-table, exactly resembling the one used by his father. The desk portion of the table shuts with a spring, and can only be opened with a golden key, which the Prince always wears on his watch chain. This room, where the Prince spends much of his time, is panelled in walnut wood.

When in London the Prince of Wales has but little time to spare, for almost every hour of his day is mapped out for him. First comes his private correspondence, which is very considerable. Then from ten to half-past ten is spent in talking over and dictating replies to the letters already sorted by Sir Francis Knollys. Immediately after, the Comptroller of the Household discusses with His Royal Highness the arrangements for the day. Often before lunch the Prince has to receive a deputation, or to act as chairman of some committee, frequently held in Marlborough House.

Luncheon is served at 2.30, and the Prince and Princess often entertain parties of their relations who are up in town for the day, for their house is the only Royal establishment now kept up in town, with the exception of York House, where, however, the Duke and Duchess of York have only a comparatively small household. Except when he is travelling, the Prince rarely has a free afternoon, for even on the rare occasions when he has not to visit some public institution, to lay a foundation-stone, or to declare a building open, and so on, there are endless social duties to which no one can attend but himself, such as weddings, race meetings, reviews, and receptions. There are certain public functions which are always attended by both the Prince and Princess—for example, the Horse Show at Islington, the Royal Military Tournament, and the trooping of the colour.

MARLBOROUGH HOUSE : THE DRAWING-ROOM
Photograph by Ralph, Dersingham

The Prince of Wales gives each season a certain number of dinners which, though in no sense official functions, take the place of those which would in other circumstances be given at Court. Thus he very often entertains various members of the Opposition as well as of the Government. He also occasionally gives what may be called a diplomatic dinner, to which a number of the foreign Ambassadors and Ministers are invited. On many occasions splendid dinner-parties in honour of a foreign guest or Royal relation passing through town in semi-*incognito* have given some favoured members of London society an opportunity of making the acquaintance of a great foreign personage. When the Shahzada was in England the Prince and Princess of Wales gave a banquet in his honour, at which covers were laid for forty. On this occasion, curiously enough, the Prince's chief guest was not able to partake of any dish in the *menu* save one entitled *riz à l'Impératrice*. However, he had brought with him his own provisions.

The dining-room in which great dinners are served at Marlborough House is a very fine apartment, containing a considerable number of their Royal Highnesses' wedding-presents. The Prince does not sit at the end of the table, as is usual in most houses, but in the middle seat opposite the buffet, his guests being on the right and left and opposite to him. Good taste reigns over all the arrangements. Thus the tablecloths are severely plain, though of the finest quality, and simply worked with the Royal arms, the rose, the thistle, and the shamrock, while the tablenapkins are invariably folded into a small square to hold the bread, and never in the fancy shapes in vogue elsewhere. To each guest two forks, and no more, are provided, and these are placed prongs downwards. In addition, there are one large tablespoon and one large knife, for in no circumstances are two knives together given to any guest. A great many reasons have been assigned for this rule, but apparently no one has summoned up the courage to ask their Royal host and hostess. It has been asserted that His Royal Highness has the old-fashioned dislike to seeing knives inadvertently crossed. Small water-bottles are used, but the Princess holds to the Hanoverian habit of never having finger-bowls.

The table decorations are quite old-fashioned, for their Royal Highnesses have remained very conservative in all their arrangements, but the flowers placed in the heavy old-world centre-piece are very beautiful, consisting often of roses and the rarest orchids. The *menu* cards are absolutely plain, with a narrow gold border and the Prince of Wales's crest. The *menu* is always printed in French, the courses being divided into a first and second service.

The Prince of Wales has never concealed his great dislike to the immensely long fatiguing banquets which were in his youth the rule rather than the exception; indeed, he may be said to have revolutionised the British dinner-party. At Marlborough House dinner begins at a quarter to nine, and is never allowed to last much over an hour. Occasionally during dinner soft music is played. The *menu* is always served à *la Russe*, that is to say, nothing is carved in the dining-room. Certain dishes are constantly met with in the *menu*, notably genuine turtle-soup, venison when in season, champagne sorbet (a kind of French ice of which both the Prince and Princess are exceedingly fond), and various sorts of salads. The wines are all decanted, and the Prince's favourite champagne is an 1889 vintage. The dessert service generally used is Royal blue Sèvres.

All the catering is done in the house, and every dinner served is prepared under the direct supervision of the Prince of Wales's *chef* (the famous Ménager), who has under him the comparatively small staff of two cooks, a confectioner, and ten kitchen-maids. But it is perhaps owing to this fact that there is no confusion in the Marlborough House kitchens, and that everything is done with celerity and perfect cleanliness. The kitchen department of Marlborough House is not without interest, for in addition to the two huge kitchens there are a number of supplementary rooms, where the different kinds of cookery from the soups to the confectionery are carried out. These are none too numerous, considering that in them the whole of the cooking is done, not only for the Prince and Princess of Wales, but also for the whole Household. Moreover, on the occasion of a garden party, the very ample refreshments provided in the long marquee on the lawn are entirely prepared " at home," and include, in addition to champagne, claret-cup, and so on, every kind of sandwich, and some half-dozen different ices.

Some years ago the Prince was rarely seen, even at dinner at a private house, without his favourite valet Macdonald, the son of the Prince Consort's *jager*; and now, whenever the Prince dines out, one of his own servants invariably accompanies him and attends to him through the dinner, whether it is a public banquet or a private dinner-party. Indeed the Prince of Wales very rarely enjoys the luxury of being alone; even when walking up St. James's Street, or turning into the Marlborough Club, he is almost invariably accom-

LIFE IN LONDON 169

panied by one of his equerries ; and it need hardly be said that the most trustworthy detectives in the London police force are charged with the task of watching over his personal safety, for the appearance of no public personage is better known to the man in the street

GARDEN PARTY AT MARLBOROUGH HOUSE, JULY 1881
From the " Illustrated London News"

than is that of the Prince of Wales. Yet, strange to say, his life has never been once attempted.

The Prince of Wales has always been an enthusiastic admirer of the stage, and his tastes are so catholic that they range from melodrama at the Adelphi to grand opera at Covent Garden. When His Royal Highness has made up his mind that he would like to go to the theatre, the Royal box is booked in the ordinary way of business, and charged to the Marlborough House account, the price not being increased from the ordinary library tariff. The only difference made in honour of the Royal family is that, if any other patron of the theatre has already engaged the Royal box, he is requested to waive his right. The Prince, however, is always reluctant that this should be done, and he generally requests his secretary to send a special note of thanks in his name.

Both the Prince and Princess always desire to be treated exactly the same as if they belonged to the ordinary audience, and nothing annoys them more than that attention should be drawn to them by the playing of the National Anthem or "God bless the Prince of Wales." At one time the managers used to keep the curtain down till the Royal party arrived. His Royal Highness heard of this, and was so much annoyed at the thought of the inconvenience thus caused to the public that he gave strict orders that the curtain was never to be kept down beyond the advertised time on his account. On the other hand, he always makes a point of waiting till the final curtain has come down before rising to leave. The only occasions on which he ever breaks this courteous rule is when he goes to a theatre which has no private entrance. Then the Prince and Princess always anticipate the final curtain by two or three minutes, so that their departure may not disturb the carriage arrangements of the rest of the audience.

London managers have reason to be grateful to the Prince of Wales, for whenever he has visited a theatre the booking sensibly increases, the more so that when His Royal Highness likes a play he goes again and again, and recommends it to all his friends. Even when he finds it impossible himself to attend the benefit of some well-known actor or actress, he always puts his name down for stalls or boxes to a substantial amount.

At the opera the Prince occupies an "omnibus," a double box on the ground tier, the Royal box itself being on the tier above; while the Princess has a box all to herself, where she is usually accompanied by one of her daughters. The Prince is a great music-lover, and always watches the progress of the opera very keenly, ensconcing himself behind the red curtain of his box so that he cannot well be seen, although he can survey the whole house through his lorgnette. He is often accompanied at the opera by the Earl of Lathom, whose long white beard is distinguishable anywhere; and he never has ladies in his box, although during the *entr'actes* he often visits the Princess and his daughter in their box.

His interest in the dramatic profession is unaffected and sincere. Some four years ago a very interesting theatrical dinner took place

MARLBOROUGH HOUSE : THE SALON
Photograph by Ralph, Dersingham

at Marlborough House, Sir Henry Irving, Sir Squire Bancroft, Mr. Hare, Mr. Kendal, Mr. Toole, Mr. Wyndham, Mr. Beerbohm Tree, Mr. Alexander, Mr. David James, Mr. Arthur Cecil, and Mr. William Farren being asked to meet the Duke of Fife, Sir Christopher Teesdale, Mr. Sala, Mr. Burnand, and Mr. Pinero.

The Prince has always patronised the French plays when performed in London, and he is as popular with the French theatrical world as he is with the dramatic profession in London.

The Prince was at one time very fond of taking a hansom in the streets of London, just like an ordinary person, and it is said that he always pays the driver half a sovereign whether the distance is long or short. His Royal Highness is patron of the Cabdrivers' Benevolent Association, and he takes a marked interest in these hard-worked and deserving servants of the public, never missing the annual meeting, at which, indeed, some of his best speeches have been delivered.

It is hardly necessary to say that the Prince of Wales need never take a hansom except for his own amusement. The stables of Marlborough House form a most important section of His Royal Highness's London establishment. They cost over £25,000, and are, from every point of view, models of what town stables ought to be. In the coach-houses are some interesting carriages. The State Coach, which is practically never used, is almost exactly like that which is kept at Buckingham Palace. A Russian sociable, lined with dark-blue morocco, was a gift from the late Tsar of Russia to the Princess of Wales, but it is considered too showy for the London streets, and Her Royal Highness prefers a light victoria, which is generally drawn by her two greys, Chelsea and Brief. The Prince's brougham, made by Hooper, is an exact facsimile of one which caught His Royal Highness's fancy in Paris many years ago. It is lined with dark blue, and is a natty unobtrusive-looking vehicle.

During the season over forty men are employed in the stables, and, as all servants in the Prince of Wales's employment are eligible for a pension after ten years' service, the competition for vacancies on the staff is keen. Every animal in the stables is taken out every day for exercise. There are forty-five stalls and twelve loose boxes, the name of each horse being inscribed on an enamel tablet over his stall. In the harness-room is a curious collection of State harness and some old saddles, together with a valuable collection of whips, chased in gold and studded with gems. All the harness, however, actually used by their Royal Highnesses is very plain.

CHAPTER XVII

PERSONAL CHARACTERISTICS

THERE is certainly no man in the whole of the British Empire about whom more widely different views have been, and are now, entertained than the Prince of Wales. His position as the Heir-Apparent of a Sovereign whom repeated bereavements have driven into retirement, which is, however, more apparent than real, has been an extremely delicate one. Nearly all his predecessors in the title of Prince of Wales played some part in politics, or interfered, not always successfully, in the affairs of State. But the idea of constitutional monarchy, which the Queen from the beginning placed before herself, is wholly inconsistent with such interference on the part of the Heir-Apparent, and His Royal Highness has most scrupulously carried out this theory of his own position.

No political party has ever been able honestly to claim the Prince of Wales as an adherent, or even as a platonic sympathiser. On the other hand, not his most severe critics have ever accused him of apathy to British interests. In that higher sphere of patriotism, which rises superior to the din of party politics, he has in every possible way earned the title of the typical Englishman.

The Prince of Wales has shown this superiority to party or sectional interests most conspicuously in his choice of those whom he has honoured with his regard and confidence. Among these, politicians are naturally numerous, but the Prince has always been most careful not to show favour to the men of one side rather than the other. Indeed, so delicate is his tact, that he is accustomed to distinguish those who happen at the moment not to be enjoying the sweets of office a little more, if anything, than those who are.

So well understood is this aloofness of his from politics, that the Prince has been able to show on many occasions the esteem and even affection in which he holds both Mr. and Mrs. Gladstone. The only time the Prince and Princess of Wales have ever been photographed together with any conspicuous popular figure was with the aged statesman and his wife, though it need hardly be added that this signal proof of friendship was given after Mr. Gladstone's final retirement from politics.

It would be wearisome to enumerate all the statesmen and politicians on whom the Prince of Wales has conferred various marks of his favour. Mention may, however, be made of Mr. Cecil Rhodes, for whom he entertains a strong admiration which he has never cared to conceal. Indeed, His Royal Highness showed such a marked interest in the famous African statesman that he removed his own name from the Travellers' Club when Mr. Rhodes was blackballed—a course which he has never seen fit to take in any other instance. His Royal Highness was naturally very much interested in the South African Committee, the earlier sittings of which he attended with great regularity.

The political emancipation of the Jews in England evidently had the Prince of Wales's warm sympathy. It now seems a long time ago since the presence of His Royal Highness at the marriage of Mr. Leopold de Rothschild caused much satisfaction and some sensation in Jewish circles, for no British prince had visited a synagogue since 1809, when three of the Royal dukes were present at a Jewish service. The Rothschild family have long been among the Prince's personal friends, both in England and on the Continent, and among his intimates was the late Baron Hirsch, with whom he stayed in Austria, notwithstanding the intense anti-Semitic feeling obtaining at the Austrian Court. The Prince of Wales has thoroughly studied the question of the Russian Jews, and has interested himself on their behalf in such a way as should earn for him the gratitude of every Jew in Europe and America. Nevertheless, the Prince's predilection for the Chosen People has been sometimes misinterpreted, and ascribed to not very creditable motives. People were at one time fond of saying that the Prince was up to the neck in debt, but, on the question being directly asked, Sir

THE PRINCE OF WALES AS COLONEL OF THE 18TH HUSSARS
From a Photograph by F.G.O.S., published by Gregory

Francis Knollys, the private secretary of the Prince, replied that the Prince had no debts worth speaking of, and that he could pay any moment every farthing he owed; also, that there was not a word of truth in the oft-repeated tales of the mortgage on Sandringham, and that the whole story was a fabrication, and was on a par with similar tales representing the Prince as being assisted by financiers of more or less doubtful honesty.

For Americans the Prince of Wales has also shown a strong liking, but it is false to assert that his favour has been confined to those American men and women whose social position has been entirely purchased by their wealth. He has frequently gone out of his way to show special courtesy to really distinguished American visitors, whether rich or poor; and the diplomatic representative of the United States in London has always found a specially cordial welcome at Marlborough House. This was particularly the case with James Russell Lowell and with Mr. T. F. Bayard. Indeed, it will be remembered that on Mr. Bayard's giving up the post of American Ambassador, the Prince broke his invariable rule and accepted Mr. Bayard's invitation to dinner, thereby paying a signal compliment to the whole American people. The Prince's telegram to the *New York World*, during the war-scare which followed President Cleveland's Venezuelan Message, will be remembered as having done much to calm the public anxiety in both countries.

American women who have married Englishmen can rely on receiving from the Prince and Princess of Wales the most tactful consideration and courtesy. This has been conspicuously shown in the cases of Lady Harcourt, the daughter of Motley, the great American historian; of Mrs. Joseph Chamberlain; and of the young Duchess of Marlborough.

The Prince of Wales has not been so often painted as his Imperial nephew, the German Emperor; in fact, he has a very great objection to sitting for his portrait. The latest portrait of him, however, was painted by Mr. Julian Story, as a commission from Mr. Astor, in order to commemorate the visit of the Prince to Clieveden. The portrait, which is life size, now hangs in the billiard-room at Clieveden, and the Prince was so much pleased with it that he has ordered a small replica for himself. Mr Frank Holt has

PERSONAL CHARACTERISTICS 177

also drawn a portrait of the Prince, as has also Edouard Detaille, the great French military painter ; but most of His Royal Highness's friends and relations much prefer the admirable portrait painted by Mr. Archibald Stuart Wortley.

There is probably not a civilised country in the world where the Prince has not at any rate some friends. With France he has many links, dating principally from the days when so much intimacy subsisted between the French and the English Courts. With the House of Orleans the Prince and Princess of Wales and their children enjoy all the intimacy of cousinship, the more so that the Princess's youngest brother, Prince Waldemar, is married to a daughter of the Duc de Chartres.

The Prince is accustomed to utilise his travels for the purpose of keeping up his old friendships and of making new ones. It is interesting to note that he speaks fluently French, German, and Italian, with a little Russian.

Of late years the Prince of Wales's brief holidays have been almost always spent on the Continent. His Royal Highness generally travels when abroad as the Earl of Chester, and sometimes as Baron Renfrew. At Boulogne a private saloon carriage is kept for the use of His Royal Highness. It was constructed by the South-Eastern Railway Company at a cost of about £7000, and cannot be kept in proper order for less than £250 a year. It contains two sleeping-apartments, a dining-car, and a study, and is painted a bright yellow, with the Prince of Wales's feathers introduced at intervals.

Few people are aware what extraordinary precautions are taken when the Prince of Wales is travelling. The general manager of the railway is always apprised of the journey beforehand by His Royal Highness's private secretary, and a notice is sent to every station-master along the line. It is not usual, as in the case of the Queen, to send a pilot engine on ahead, but on the whole the line is kept clear ; and a train containing the Prince of Wales is never allowed to go more than fifty miles an hour. This care is taken just as much when the Prince is travelling in an ordinary express as when he has ordered a special.

It has sometimes been asserted that members of the Royal family travel free of expense. This is a mistake. Travelling is one of the heaviest items in the Prince of Wales's annual expenditure, the more so that both he and the Princess are very lavish in the matter of tips.

Many stories are told in Paris of the Prince's experiences with persons who were quite unaware that they were addressing the *Prince de Galles*. On one occasion, when His Royal Highness and an equerry were going through the Louvre galleries they were observed by a party of Americans, one of whom remarked in a loud whisper to one of his friends, " I'll bet you ten naps that's the Prince of Wales."—" Done," cried the other. Accordingly, a few moments later the American approached the Prince's equerry and asked him in low tone the name of his companion. " The Earl of Chester," was the truthful answer. "Sold," said the Yankee in a disappointed tone.

It is not generally known that the Princess of Wales shares her husband's liking for Paris, and together they have spent some happy days in the gay city. The faces of the Princess and her daughters are naturally not so familiar in Paris as they are in London, and this has enabled their Royal Highnesses to take several walks along the Boulevards and in the main thoroughfares without being recognised by the crowd. On one occasion the Prince and Princess dined at the Elysée with President Grévy and his wife and daughter. There is no doubt that this dinner-party must have been in some ways the most remarkable ever attended by their Royal Highnesses, for, though they were treated with respect, none of the etiquette of courts was attempted. Thus, the ladies sat down in the presence of the Princess before dinner was announced. The Prince took in Madame la Présidente, while the aged President escorted the Princess to a seat on his right hand.

When in Paris, the Prince of Wales, whether alone or accompanied by any member of his family, always stays at the Hôtel Bristol, a stately hostelry situated on the Place Vendôme. He always occupies the same suite of apartments, and he is rarely seen in any of the public rooms of the hotel.

It is characteristic of the Prince's discretion and good sense that when he is abroad he never attends, as do many of his country-

PERSONAL CHARACTERISTICS 179

THE DUKE OF CONNAUGHT AND THE PRINCE OF WALES
From a Photograph by F.G.O.S., published by Gregory.

men, any race-meetings on Sundays. On one occasion, many years ago, when he was still quite a young man, he received a special invitation from Marshal MacMahon to accompany him to the Grand Prix. He telegraphed to the Queen for permission, but Her Majesty returned a reply in the negative, and the Prince resigned himself to disappointing the famous French soldier.

His Royal Highness speaks French perfectly, and can make as good a speech in Paris as he can in London. On one occasion a French lady asked the Prince why he did not settle in France. "Vous usez vos rois trop vite dans ce pays," was the witty retort.

Of late years the Prince has spent a certain portion of each winter in the South of France. He makes his headquarters at Cannes, the great yachting centre of the Riviera ; and those who picture him spending his days and nights at Monte Carlo have formed a very erroneous opinion of their future King's character and tastes. A little reflection would surely show that, apart from other reasons, it would be impossible for so well known a Royal personage to do more than stroll through the famous gambling-rooms ; even as it is, the Prince cannot show himself in any place of public entertainment without being more or less discreetly mobbed by the ill-bred majority of those present, and it would be out of the question for him to take up his stand for any time either at a *roulette* or a *trente et quarante* table.

Another Continental resort which has often had the honour of entertaining the Prince of Wales is Homburg. When undergoing the "cure" in the pretty German Spa, His Royal Highness sets an excellent example to his fellow-patients. He always stays at Ritter's Hotel, rises at six, and walks down to the Elizabeth Well, where the healing water is handed to him in a quaintly-shaped glass on a silver salver. After drinking two or three glasses of the sparkling waters, he walks off with some friend, either to the beautiful park or into the country beyond to the lovely fir-wood known as the Grosser Tannenwald. Cronberg, the Empress Frederick's beautiful home in the Taunus Mountains, is within a drive of Homburg, and when he is there the Prince often pays his favourite sister a visit. Having revived the glories of Homburg, the Prince has more recently sought rest and quiet at the smaller spa of Marienbad.

CHAPTER XVIII

PERSONAL CHARACTERISTICS—*continued*

ONE of the most absorbing interests of the Prince of Wales's life is undoubtedly the ancient craft of Freemasonry. And yet very few foreign princes are Masons; and, though the Duke of Kent was one, the Prince Consort always refused to associate himself with the craft. Of course it must be remembered that British Freemasonry is a very different thing from what the term is supposed to imply on the Continent, where it is associated in the public mind with atheism and even anarchism.

The Prince of Wales was initiated into the mysteries of Freemasonry in Sweden in 1868 by the late King. He was elected Grand Master of England in succession to the Marquis of Ripon, who resigned in 1875. The scene in the Albert Hall at his installation was very striking. The platform usually occupied by the choir was then transformed into a daïs, on which the throne was placed, the space around being large enough for four or five hundred Provincial Grand Masters, Past Grand Officers, and visitors of distinction. The throne was the one in which George IV. was installed when he was Prince of Wales. It was covered with rich purple velvet, and the floor was laid with a magnificent Oriental carpet, a century old, lent for the occasion by a member of the Westminster and Keystone Lodge. Behind the throne the banner of Grand Lodge and other flags were placed; in front a wide aisle was formed right across the area to the Royal entrance. This was laid with a rich carpet of velvet pile, woven expressly for the occasion. The ground was blue, enriched alternately with the arms of Grand Lodge and Prince of Wales's feathers.

After the formalities of installation were completed, His Royal Highness, as Grand Master, was received with enthusiastic applause. When returning thanks to his brethren for the high honour they had that day bestowed upon him, the Prince said that it was an honour which several members of his family had borne, and he wished to follow in their steps, and, by God's grace, to fulfil the duties of his office as they had done.

Although His Royal Highness has long been an active Freemason, it was only a few years ago that he had at the same moment the disposition and the opportunity to attend the consecration of a Lodge in his official capacity as Grand Master of England. That occasion was the consecration of the Chancery Bar Lodge of Freemasons in Lincoln's Inn Hall. The Prince sat in the Grand Master's chair, wearing the full regalia of his office; at his left sat the Earl of Lathom, Pro-Grand Master, and at his right, the Earl of Mount-Edgcumbe, Deputy Grand Master.

Many curious incidents have occurred in connection with the Prince's interest in Freemasonry. At one dinner at which the King of Sweden was present, the list of subscriptions announced amounted to the enormous sum of £51,000, the largest amount ever raised at a festival dinner in the history of the world. When the Prince of Wales laid the first stone of Truro Cathedral with full Masonic honours, the mallet used by him was the one with which Charles II. laid the foundation-stone of St. Paul's Cathedral. It was presented to the old Lodge of St. Paul by Sir Christopher Wren, who was a member.

On two occasions His Royal Highness has presided as Grand Master of the English Freemasons over a magnificent assembly at the Royal Albert Hall. The first was in celebration of the Queen's Jubilee in 1887, when the tickets for admission produced £6000, a sum which was divided among the three great Masonic charities. Very similar was the Diamond Jubilee assembly of Freemasons, at which eight thousand members were present. The Prince of Wales spoke admirably, the Duke of Connaught moving the adoption of the address to the Queen, while Lord Amherst aroused unbounded enthusiasm when he alluded to Her Majesty as "the daughter of a Freemason, the mother of Freemasons, and the patron and benefactress of our Order."

As may be imagined from the diversity of his interests, as well as from his position so near the throne, the Prince of Wales's correspondence has of late years rivalled that of the Queen, and His Royal Highness is always eager to acknowledge the debt he owes to his hard-working and clever groom-in-waiting and private secretary, Sir Francis Knollys, on whom falls much of the responsibility connected with the Prince's letter-bag. Sir Francis occupies a pretty suite of rooms in St. James's Palace, close to Marlborough House, and his study is in communication with the Prince's private apartments; but most of his work is actually transacted at Marlborough House, for every morning he makes his way across and attacks the vast piles of letters laid out for his inspection.

The Prince's correspondence is then reduced by his private secretary to three distinct sections—the private letters, the business letters, and the miscellaneous letters. Among the latter are those written by lunatics, begging-letter writers, and so on. The private letters are sent up to the Prince unopened, the others are all read through by Sir Francis and again subdivided, the larger section to be replied to in a formal and official way, the others to be submitted to the Prince before they are dealt with.

Some of His Royal Highness's correspondents evidently have a touching belief in his power of righting wrong. They implore him to take up their cause when they are injured, and it may be stated that no *bona fide* epistle is ever sent to Marlborough House addressed to the Prince of Wales without being answered, often with marvellous celerity, and ever with the greatest courtesy and kindness.

As to the vast masses of begging letters, it is no secret that the Prince of Wales has been from the first a consistent supporter of the Charity Organisation Society; and long before the excellent work done by that Society was as widely recognised as it is now, the Prince saw its infinite possibilities for good, and became a regular subscriber to the Mendicity Society, as it was then styled. Accordingly, His Royal Highness has rarely been imposed on even by the cleverest *chevaliers d'industrie*. On the other hand, he is genuinely charitable, and on several occasions known to the writer has exerted himself privately to obtain pensions and grants of money for deserving individuals who had fallen on evil times.

At Sandringham there is a post office inside the house for the use of the Royal Household, but at Marlborough House the huge letter-bags are sent over to the St. James's Street post office at regular intervals throughout the day.

The Prince has long been a subscriber to the National Telephone Company, and he is said to spend over £1000 a year in telegrams

SIR FRANCIS KNOLLYS
From a Photograph by Russell

alone, for the popular idea that Royalty's letters are franked, and that parcels sent by them are forwarded free of cost, is a delusion.

Sir Francis Knollys's duties as secretary are not confined to what are generally called secretarial duties. He has to act as his Royal master's supplementary memory. He keeps the list of all the Prince's engagements, and, what is a more arduous task, arranges every item of the Royal journeys. Princess Charles of Denmark is

PERSONAL CHARACTERISTICS 185

said to have once observed that she felt sure that if Sir Francis were suddenly awakened in the middle of the night and asked what were the Prince of Wales's engagements eight days forward, he would immediately begin to recite the entire list.

Be that as it may, the position of Sir Francis Knollys is a very responsible one, and even his most intimate friends marvel how he can get through the enormous amount of work he has to do. Occasionally his labours are enormously increased. At times of public calamity or Royal mourning, thousands and thousands of letters and telegrams pour into both Marlborough House and Sandringham, all requiring some kind of attention, and in most cases an immediate answer. During the Tranby Croft case well-intentioned folk all over the British Empire sent books and pamphlets pointing out the evils of gambling, and in most cases these were courteously and kindly acknowledged.

Sir Francis writes every important letter with his own hand, for typewriters have, so far, never been used in Royal correspondence. He has two assistant secretaries who attend to the routine work, but even then many of the letters written by them are signed by him, and in all cases he looks them over and sees that they are as he would wish them to be. There is also a staff of clerks, who are absolutely pledged never to reveal anything they may learn about the private affairs of the Prince and Princess, or indeed of the Royal family as a whole.

Few people realise how large a portion of their income is given away each year by the Prince and Princess of Wales in charity. During the last thirty years the aggregate amount given away by their Royal Highnesses represents a large fortune. Whenever one of those great calamities which strike the imagination of large sections of the British people occurs, one of the first contributions to any fund raised is generally sent from Marlborough House. Then, again, the presence of the Prince or the Princess at a philanthropic gathering is sure to bring in, directly or indirectly, a large sum of money to the undertaking. For instance, on the first occasion when the Prince and Princess appeared together in support of a charity— the British Orphan Asylum at Slough—one gentleman announced that he would contribute £12,000.

The greatest care has to be taken both by the Prince and the Princess in selecting the tradesmen upon whom they will confer the undoubted advantage of their custom. Sir Dighton Probyn, the Comptroller of the Prince of Wales's Household, plays a very great part in His Royal Highness's life, for it is thanks to him that the Prince's London establishment is so admirably organised and managed. It is his duty to see that the Prince's Warrants are only given to those who are worthy of them. A Royal Warrant is naturally considered a great honour by the recipient, and any firm aspiring to be a Warrant-Holder must supply the Prince of Wales's Household for one year in a satisfactory manner before becoming eligible ; and should the firm become bankrupt, or even change its name, the Warrant must be returned to the Comptroller of the Household.

On the Prince's birthday the Warrant-Holders are wont to dine together, and on the *menu* always figures some venison contributed both by the Queen and by the Prince of Wales, who each send a fine buck. On all Royal occasions of rejoicing the Warrant-Holders are considered to have a special right to present a gift accompanied by their congratulations.

Every monetary transaction is not only recorded, but indexed at Marlborough House ; and it is a significant fact that any tradesman who sends in an account twice over is never again patronised by their Royal Highnesses.

His Royal Highness does not confine his custom to any one London tailor ; on the contrary, he is careful to distribute his patronage, and it is a mistake to fancy that His Royal Highness pays very much more for his clothes than do other people. His wardrobe is necessarily larger and more varied than that of a private individual. It need hardly be said that he dresses in perfect taste, and it is well known that he has no sympathy with the revolutionists who would abolish the frock-coat. His Royal Highness is, however, also understood to have a special fondness for the old-fashioned "bowler" hat. It would be difficult to over-estimate the Prince's influence as an arbiter of fashion, especially in America, where every trifling change in his costume is faithfully reported and imitated, and also on the Continent. On the whole, his influence in matters of

THE PRINCE AS ADMIRAL
From a Photograph by Russell

dress is strongly conservative. He has none of the Continental love of displaying uniforms, and his dress is always the acme of good taste, because it is always absolutely suitable to the occasion on which it is worn.

The Prince has an ever-increasing number of uniforms, military and other. Every one of his honorary army titles requires four complete uniforms,—full dress, undress, mess dress, and overcoat. His uniforms and robes are worth quite £15,000, and are, of course, fully insured.

It need hardly be said that the Prince has almost every Order in existence. The mere enumeration of them fills up a large space in Debrett. Some of them are extremely valuable. The principal Order possessed by His Royal Highness is, of course, the Garter, which is only worn by him on great occasions. The badge consists of a dark blue velvet garter edged with gold, with gold buckle and pendant, and bearing the motto, *Honi soit qui mal y pense*. His Royal Highness is very fond of wearing the Collar of the Bath, of which he is now Great Master. The actual Order itself consists of a Maltese cross, a collar of gold, a star, a habit, and a crimson riband.

The Prince's own favourite among his Orders is that of Malta, the Sovereign Order of St. John of Jerusalem, of which the badge is the well-known Maltese cross suspended from a black ribbon. When in Scotland, His Royal Highness wears on State occasions the Order of the Thistle, of which the badge is a figure of St. Andrew in enamelled gold, bearing a St. Andrew's cross, surrounded by golden rays terminating in eight principal points in the form of a glory.

When the Prince of Wales is in Paris he generally wears the rosette of an officer of the Legion of Honour. This enables him, when walking about the town *incognito*, to pass unchallenged anywhere and everywhere.

Mr. John Porter and Mr. Richard Marsh, the Prince's Past and Present Trainers, and John Watts, his Jockey

From Photographs by Elliott & Fry, and Clarence Hailey

CHAPTER XIX

THE PRINCE AS A SPORTSMAN—THE TURF—PERSIMMON'S DERBY—
THE DERBY-DAY DINNER — HUNTING — SHOOTING — DEER-
STALKING—YACHTING.

THE Prince of Wales has always taken a very keen interest in those sports and pastimes which are peculiarly British, and perhaps it is to this that he owes his remarkable bodily vigour and healthy appearance, for he is never so content as when enjoying a long day's tramp over the stubble at Sandringham, or when deer-stalking in a soft Highland mist.

His Royal Highness's life as a sportsman began early. When he was quite a child he used to accompany Prince Albert on deer-stalking expeditions round Balmoral; somewhat later he hunted with the harriers; and when he was fifteen he could claim to be the best shot in his family. But of late years the Prince of Wales has been rather associated in the public mind with the sport of kings, and the Royal colours—purple, gold band, scarlet sleeves, and black velvet cap with gold fringe—are a familiar sight on most British race-courses. Although the Prince has been a member of the

Jockey Club for thirty years, his keen personal interest in racing is a matter of later growth, for it was not till July 1877 that the Princess of Wales honoured Newmarket with her presence to see her husband's colours carried for the first time. On that occasion the Prince had no luck, although Alep, a pure-bred Arab, started favourite, being, however, beaten by Lord Strathnairn's Arab Avowal by twenty or thirty lengths. Five years later the Prince won the Household Brigade Cup at Sandown with Fairplay.

In 1890 His Royal Highness put his racers under John Porter, but his total winnings were only £624. The next year the Prince won £4148; in 1892, £190; in 1893, £372; in 1894, £3499; and in 1895, £8281; and in the last-named year His Royal Highness's name stood tenth in the list of winning owners. This satisfactory result was undoubtedly greatly owing to Lord Marcus Beresford, who was entrusted with the management of the Prince's racing stable in 1890.

The Prince of Wales is generally agreed to be a very good judge of a horse. When at Newmarket he makes it a point to watch the early morning gallops, and at one time he was very fond of attending sales. The Prince has also given a great impetus to horse-breeding in the United Kingdom. Many years ago he started a thorough-bred stud, a half-bred stud, and a shire-horse stud—works of real public utility, which can only be undertaken, be it remembered, by those who have wealth and leisure, combined with intelligence and a real desire to forward the interests of the British farmer.

Of late the Prince has had the satisfaction of seeing his colours often pass the winning-post, but it need hardly be said that his greatest triumph was the victory of Persimmon in the Derby of 1896. This fine horse—a bay by St. Simon, and own brother to Florizel II., who was, by the way, the first really good horse that ever carried the Royal colours—is a magnificent specimen of the thorough-bred. Persimmon has never been beaten by any horse except his own half-brother, St. Frusquin. He was bred by the Prince of Wales and trained by Marsh at Newmarket. He made his first appearance in the Coventry Stakes at Ascot as a two-year-old,

PERSIMMON

and, starting favourite, won the race. On the occasion of his next appearance, in the Richmond Stakes at Goodwood, he was again favourite, and again won by a length. In the Middle Park Plate, though favourite, he was beaten by St. Frusquin, but in the Derby of 1896 he beat his half-brother by a neck. At the Newmarket First July Meeting he gave 3 lb. to St. Frusquin, and was beaten in

THE EGERTON HOUSE TRAINING STABLES, NEWMARKET

From a Photograph by Clarence Hailey

the Princess of Wales's Stakes. He won the St. Leger by a length and a half; and in the Jockey Club Stakes at Newmarket on the 1st October he won by two lengths from Sir Visto, the Derby winner of 1897.

Persimmon was ridden to victory in the Derby of 1896 by John Watts. The race was witnessed by an extraordinarily large concourse of all classes, including a considerable number of distinguished foreigners. Never was there a more popular victory,

THE PRINCE'S DERBY, 1896

DERBY-DAY DINNER

and the enthusiasm all over the country was as great as at Epsom. It was the fourth time in the history of the Turf that the great race had been won by a Royal owner. In 1788, eight years after its foundation, the Prince Regent won with Sir Thomas; and the Duke of York won with Prince Leopold in 1816, and with Moses in 1822.

The Derby-Day dinner is certainly one of the most important functions held at Marlborough House during the year, and it is now difficult to believe that it was only inaugurated just ten years ago. Something like fifty invitations are sent out, and the guests, who are, it need hardly be said, all men, assemble in the great drawing-room, where they are joined by their Royal host just before dinner, which is announced at half-past eight. The company are expected to wear evening dress—not uniform—and the Royal guests, of whom there are as a rule from eight to ten, have each an attendant told off to wait on him, while each couple of the others present share an attendant.

On Derby Day the great silver dinner-service ordered by the Prince on his marriage, which cost some £20,000, is always used. The table is laid quite plainly, flowers being conspicuous by their absence; but on the side buffet, which exactly faces the spot where the Prince sits, are to be seen the racing-cups, the hunting-trophies, and the gold and silver salvers, for everything in the strong-room which is associated with sport is brought out for that one day.

One typical Derby dinner *menu* was as follows :—

POTAGES.

Tortue Claire.
Turtle Punch.   Bisque d'Écrevisses.

POISSONS.

Madeira, 1820.   Petites Truites au bleu, sauce Génoise.
Steinberg Cabinet, 1857.   Filets de Soles à la Norvégienne.

ENTRÉES.

Côtelettes de Cailles à la Clamart.
Chauds Froids de Volailles à la Renaissance.

THE PRINCE OF WALES

Moët et Chandon.

Still Sillery, 1846.

Chambertin, 1875.

RELEVÉS.

Hanches de Venaison, sauce aigre douce.
Mouton poêle au Champagne.
Sorbets à l'Italienne.

RÔTS.

Poussins rôtis sur canapés.
Salade de Romaine à la Française.

ENTREMÊTS.

Asperges en branches, sauce Mousseline.
Croutes aux Fraises à la Princesse.
Chartreuse de Pêches à la Montreueil.
Gradins de Patisseries Assorties.

RELEVÉS.

Casolettes de Fromage à la Russe.

GLACE.

Buissons de Glaces à la Napolitaine.

Royal tawny port, 50 years old.
Royal white port.
Sherry, George IV.
Magnums, Château Lafite, 1864.
Brandy, 1848.

When dinner is over, His Royal Highness gives a signal for smoking to begin, then an adjournment is made to the large drawing-room, where tables are found set out for cards.

Although the Prince of Wales has been a plucky and fearless rider from early childhood, he has never been specially identified with the hunting-field, and during the last few years he has seldom been seen following the hounds. When an undergraduate at Christ Church, he constantly hunted with Lord Macclesfield's pack, and was then considered a very hard rider; and it need hardly be said that the meets which take place at Sandringham are the most popular in Norfolk, and give both the Prince and Princess of Wales many opportunities of showing gracious and kindly hospitality, both to their wealthy and their humble neighbours.

Before the Prince had been at Sandringham six months he made it quite clear that his country home should be in every sense a good sporting estate, and it has been one of His Royal Highness's chief pleasures to entertain parties of keen sportsmen each autumn in Norfolk. It is on record that the best shooting season Sandringham has ever seen was that of 1885-86. The total bag was 16,131 head, including 7252 pheasants. The best day of that season was the last day of the year 1885, when ten guns killed 2835 head, including 1275 pheasants. The rabbit-shooting at Sandringham is also first-rate, and it need hardly be said that the foxes are watched over with the most tender anxiety, the covers being said to be among the best in the country.

Over ten thousand pheasants are annually reared at Sandringham, partly by incubators and partly by the assistance of a thousand ordinary hens. The lake near Sandringham affords wild duck, teal, and widgeon shooting. The Prince has the largest game-room in the United Kingdom. It holds between six and seven thousand head, and was built not very long after the Prince bought the estate. After each day's sport the game is spread for inspection, and a careful record is made of the numbers that have fallen to each gun. It is in the game-room that the game is packed after a big *battue* to be sent off in hampers to hospitals and to friends. It need hardly be said that none of the Prince's game is ever sold. A good deal is kept for the use of the house, and a share is also given to the tenants, to the *employés* on the estate, and to London tradesmen connected with the Prince's Household.

The Prince's shooting-parties rarely number more than ten guns, each of whom is assigned his place in the shoot by his Royal host himself. All the beaters at Sandringham wear a very becoming uniform composed of a Royal blue blouse, low crowned hat, and long brown gaiters. Each bears on his left arm a number by which he may readily be identified, and after each day's shooting every one of the beaters is allowed to take home a hare and a pheasant.

The Prince of Wales is not often seen going north for the opening weeks of the grouse-shooting season. Still, in the early years of his married life, he and the Princess often entertained shooting-parties at Birkhall. The Prince generally puts in a certain number of days pheasant-shooting in Windsor Great Park. The preserves swarm with ground game. The Prince is entitled to take what game he requires, and all the members of the Royal family have a certain

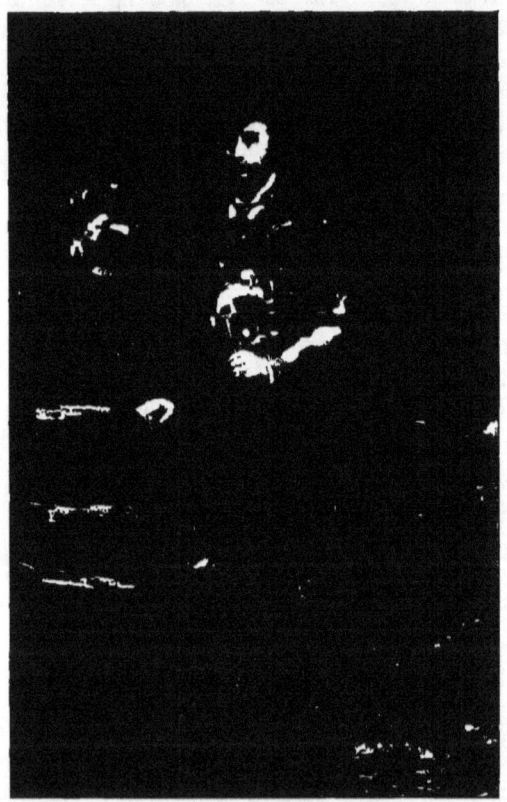

THE PRINCE AS A SPORTSMAN IN 1876
From an Engraving published by Henry Graves and Co.

quantity despatched to them, the remainder being distributed. The Prince is also fond of shooting at Wynyard, Lord Londonderry's seat in Durham. The Prince of Wales has, however, shot more or less all over England. He was frequently the guest of Lord James of Hereford when the latter had Shoreham Place, where one valley on

DEER-STALKING—YACHTING

the farther side of the park is locally known as "The Valley of the Shadow of Death," from the tremendous slaughter of game that annually takes place there.

Like his father, the late Prince Consort, the Prince of Wales has always been a keen deer-stalker, and when he is staying at Balmoral most of his time is entirely devoted to this sport—in fact, deer-stalking is what first brought him into close connection with his present son-in-law, then the Earl of Fife, who possesses Mar, one of the two largest forests in Great Britain, extending as it does to over 80,000 acres of cleared ground.

Balmoral, which, it is said, will ultimately become the property in turn of every reigning sovereign, is situated in the heart of the deer country, being within reach of a good number of forests adjoining each other, and extending without a break into five counties.

His Royal Highness is well known to prefer "stalking" to driving, but of late years he has taken an active part in the drives organised at Mar. The Prince's marksmanship is universally agreed to be excellent. His Royal Highness does not either own or rent a single acre of land in Scotland. At one time he was owner of Birkhall, in Glenmuick, but it was purchased for him by Prince Albert, and he had no voice in its selection. Still the Prince kept it till 1885, when he sold the property, which was very extensive, to the Queen.

The Prince of Wales has been extremely fortunate as a yachtsman, and probably one of the annual events to which he most looks forward each year is the Regatta at Cowes. The Prince first won the Queen's Cup, annually presented to the Royal Yacht Squadron at Cowes, in 1877, with his schooner *Hildegarde* of 198 tons. He won the Cup again in 1880 with the *Formosa*, cutter, of 103 tons, and again in 1895 and 1897 with the famous cutter *Britannia* of 151 tons.

The Royal Yacht Squadron, as is well known, was founded as "The Yacht Club" so far back as 1815. It early enjoyed the patronage of Royalty, among the past and present members being numbered the Prince Regent (afterwards George IV.), the Duke of Clarence (afterwards William IV.), the Queen, the Prince Consort, the Tsar Nicholas I., Napoleon III., the German Emperor, and Prince Henry of Prussia. The Prince of Wales became Commodore in 1882 on the death of Lord Wilton.

The Prince generally takes the chair at the annual dinner of the Squadron held at the old castle at West Cowes, built as a fort by Henry VIII., which became the headquarters of the club in 1858. This festivity is the great event of the year for all well-known

THE "BRITANNIA"

From a Photograph by Adamson, Rothesay

yachtsmen. There is a great display of plate, including the Queen's Cup, the Nelson Vase, and the beautiful model of the *Speranza*, which once belonged to Lord Conyngham. His Royal Highness presented a few years ago twenty-one cannon to the club-house at Cowes. They were taken by him from the *Royal Adelaide*, the toy warship placed by William IV. to guard the artificial ocean of Virginia Water. Now they are used for firing salutes.

It need hardly be said that the Prince is the owner of many splendid prizes won at Cowes and elsewhere. Both he and the

YACHTING 199

Princess are extremely fond of the sea, and he early made himself acquainted with the less technical side of navigation. The Prince of Wales is very fond of spending a certain number of days each year at Cannes, and when he is there in April he generally takes an active part in the Battle of Flowers; and he entertains large parties of his English and foreign friends on board the *Britannia*.

THE PRINCE IN YACHTING COSTUME
Photograph by Debenham, Cowes

www.ingramcontent.com/pod-product-compliance
Lightning Source LLC
Chambersburg PA
CBHW031818220426
43662CB00007B/698